THE
VISUAL
SALE

To helping businesses
succeed through video!

THE
VISUAL
SALE

HOW *to* USE VIDEO *to* EXPLODE SALES,
DRIVE MARKETING, *and* GROW YOUR BUSINESS
in a VIRTUAL WORLD

MARCUS SHERIDAN
TYLER LESSARD

IDEAPRESS
PUBLISHING

CONTENTS

PREFACE

To get the most out of this work, there are a few essential things you should know before reading.

You see, there is plenty of content online these days about "how to do video" as a company. There is very, very little, however, on how to truly grow your business, your brand, and your bottom line through this powerful medium.

As the authors of this work, Tyler Lessard and I (Marcus Sheridan) didn't want to produce another guide to vlogging, Instagram, or the like. Instead, we wanted to show you exactly what has been proven to get real results by real companies doing some incredible (and attainable) things with video.

Our first goal is that you're flooded with ideas as to what video could do for your organization—be it sales, marketing, or the customer experience.

Our second goal is that, upon finishing this book, you will have all of the basic tools, foundational knowledge, and direction you need to take action.

Fact is, unless you take action on what you learn through reading this, we will have all failed. This is also why we've developed a robust series of further training videos and templates at **www.thevisualsale.com**. We invite you to explore them and, most of all, use them.

It's important to note that writing a book on video isn't easy. Words will not do nearly enough justice to fully *show* the many types of videos that are discussed within these pages. Nor would it ever make sense for us to do a deep-dive on technical things like equipment, video tools, or other tech due to an ever-evolving industry. So if you'd like to learn about these things, and get our most recent recommendations on each, simply visit **www.thevisualsale.com**.

Finally, whether your company is business-to-business (B2B), business-to-consumer (B2C), services- or products-based, large or small—the principles and practices you will learn about in the following pages **will apply** to your situation, as they have proven themselves to be universal.

After all, what we're really talking about in this book is **trust.**

That's it.

Trust is the building block for all businesses, no matter industry or size. In this case, we're just discussing how to generate more trust with video. So please be open to the possibilities. Just because it has never been done before within your industry doesn't mean you can't be the first.

Finally, because we're so serious as to your ongoing success, we want to welcome your feedback and questions.

You can reach Tyler at **tyler.lessard@vidyard.com** and you'll find me at **marcus@marcussheridan.com**.

Here's to "showing it" better than anyone has ever shown it before...

An Introduction by Marcus Sheridan

YOU ARE A
MEDIA COMPANY

A few years ago, as I sat contemplating the ever-evolving buyer of today and the general inability of businesses to adapt quickly to this movement, my mind became centered on this thought:

 Video is a fundamental part of the buying process, and yet most businesses did not seem to know how to deal with the shift.

It's not that businesses didn't see the power of video. Rather the idea of video production—at least in-house—seemed completely unattainable to them. And, time and time again, I saw a pattern of businesses making the same mistakes.

They would spend thousands and thousands of dollars to hire a video production company, only to walk away with a couple of videos, a gaping hole in their marketing budget, and not much else to show for it.

Having the firm belief in the fact that the future of digital for businesses is the ability to produce the majority of their own content (without the need of outside help), I posed the following question to our team at IMPACT, my digital sales and marketing agency:

"Can we teach companies how to create a culture of video in-house? One that starts with the sales team and can be done without them needing to outsource anything?"

The reactions to my question were mixed:

"Marcus, that's never been done before."

"If we're not producing videos for our clients, how could it be a viable business model for us as an agency?"

"Most companies will fail if they do this themselves."

I pushed back again:

"Why not? Why couldn't we be the first firm to truly 'teach' organizations how to embrace a culture of video in-house? And why couldn't more sales (and marketing) teams start catching the incredible power of this medium? This is obviously where the world is headed and so what if no one else is doing it? It's what's needed. And it's the right thing to do."

With that, an incredible journey began. We threw ourselves into video and decided to teach it just as we had taught inbound sales and content marketing in my first book, *They Ask, You Answer*—start with sales in mind, and the rest will fall into place.

And fall into place it did.

Today, hundreds of clients around the globe have embraced a true culture of video within their organization.

It turns out that I wasn't alone in thinking that companies wanted to control their digital destinies, and there *was* a market for it. A lot of business owners and CEOs felt exactly as I did—that in-house ownership of video would be critical to their success in the years that lie ahead.

Even better, video is the ultimate expression of *They Ask, You Answer*. Buyers want it. And not only do they want it, but more and more they are demonstrating a clear preference to learn visually over simply reading a textual explanation.

In the following pages, we're going to answer three major questions about video:

- What types of videos actually get results from a sales and marketing perspective?
- What are some B2B and B2C case studies of companies having exceptional success using video?
- What must a company do to create a culture of in-house video that is built to last?

Keep in mind, we won't be able to answer all of your questions here. We will, however, give you a clear sense as to what proven actions and steps you can take right now within your business to see quick, powerful, and even extraordinary results from video.

PART I

WELCOME TO THE VISUAL AGE

A Note from Tyler Lessard

I haven't always been the "video-for-business guy."

In fact, I have no formal training in film or media, and when I joined Vidyard as vice president of marketing, I had no idea how to create or publish online videos. While I've long been a big advocate for video in marketing, it wasn't until I started recording and editing my own personal content that I truly appreciated its full potential.

It was the summer of 2017 when LinkedIn announced support for video content.

LinkedIn had always been an important networking channel for me, and I knew video would quickly take over as it had on Facebook and Twitter. But to start posting videos consistently on my feed as Vidyard's VP of marketing, I knew that I had to reduce my dependency on our in-house video producer before my demands became too much.

So, I learned how to capture "good enough" content with my smartphone, webcam, and GoPro. My two oldest children (eight and 10 years old at the time) taught me the basics of video editing in iMovie—which was a very humbling experience, I might add!

I bought a license to a stock music library and graduated from iMovie to Camtasia, a more advanced editing tool. I started experimenting with short videos at home to share with friends and family in addition to creating content for my social channels.

Amazingly, it didn't take long for video creation to feel natural, efficient, **and** *incredibly fun.*

Then it happened.

In early 2018, Marketo (now an Adobe company) launched the Fearless 50 awards program to recognize the most innovative and fearless marketing professionals around the world. To apply for the award, nominees had to share a video on social media explaining why they deserved this recognition.

As I started reviewing submissions from other nominees, I noticed they all followed a similar format: An individual in their office or home, on a webcam, logically explaining why they deserved to win.

They were all great stories, but very few made a lasting impression and none were particularly memorable. I knew there was an opportunity to leverage the real power of video to *show*, rather than just tell, how I'm a fearless marketer.

To create a video that my eight- and 10-year old children would be proud of.

So, I downloaded clips from some of our best marketing videos and captured screen recordings of our top campaigns. I found the instrumental version of the Imagine Dragons song "Whatever it Takes" to act as the hook for my video.

Then, I recorded my own lyrics to describe how I was willing to do *whatever it takes* to generate new leads as a marketer—and let's be clear, a singer I am not. In fact, my singing was really, really bad.

Still, I mashed it all together and unapologetically put myself out there with a one-minute video that made people laugh, applaud, and share.

Did it take more than an hour or my time to create? *Yes.*

Did I enjoy every minute of it? *You bet.*

Did I earn my way onto the Fearless 50 list and get my face plastered on a 30-foot billboard in San Francisco? *I sure did.*

Using video in a creative way to show rather than tell, to entertain my audience, and to be truly authentic made all the difference. And what

I've held onto until this day is that I did it with something that I created myself with no budget, a little creativity, and yes, a dash of fearlessness.

Thus began the latest phase of my journey as not only a video marketing and video selling strategist, but as a video creator who uses visual storytelling to connect with my audience.

Because fundamentally, the business world is all about connections.

It's the most important lesson I've learned during my career as an engineer, a business development executive, and now a marketing leader at Vidyard.

When I say "connections," I don't mean who you know or how big your following is. I mean real personal connections built on emotional resonance, and earning the most coveted prize of all from your colleagues, prospects, and customers: *trust.*

Every great sales rep knows the power of connection and trust. If someone knows you, likes you, and trusts you, they are much more likely to buy from you.

However, in an increasingly virtual world, we can no longer rely on face-to-face meetings, phone calls, or static content to build relationships. And, as we all know far too well, in times of crisis — when social distancing and travel restrictions are a reality — digital channels may be the only option we have for engaging clients in a truly personal manner

And, if there's anything I've learned in my six years at Vidyard—a provider of video hosting, creation, and analytics tools for businesses—it's that video is the next best thing to being there in person when it comes to creating connections and earning trust.

I partnered with Marcus on writing this book to share what I've learned about the power of video as a content format, and how it can be used by any business to grow faster in the digital age.

We share a passion for video's unique ability to create connections between buyer and seller. We bring a wide range of collective experience from helping hundreds of businesses implement video marketing and video selling strategies.

Most of all, we share the belief that the most valuable ideas are those you can implement quickly today, with no additional budget, to transform how you do business tomorrow.

Chapter 1

WHY VIDEO WORKS

It's no secret that people love to watch videos.

But the reasons *why* we find that play button is so irresistible—and the ways in which we can use it to fuel growth—may not be so obvious.

Ever since television found its way into our homes in the 1950s, video has been the next best thing to being there in person when it comes to how people prefer to learn, share ideas, and be entertained.

Video is a window into countless stories, a first-hand view of major events, and an instant gateway to knowledge and learning. And—if you look at how younger generations are consuming, creating, and sharing video—it's only going to become even more pervasive in both our personal and business lives.

In fact, I'm lucky enough to have my own focus group on this topic in the comfort of my own home: four *digital and video natives* (AKA children) between the ages of four and 12 years old. Each and every day I bear witness to how different their content consumption behaviors have become compared to when I was growing up.

There was one day in particular when this became all too clear to me. In fact, it made me pause and wonder if I should even be writing this book!

I was in my study working on this very manuscript when my 10-year-old son, Alec, popped in to see what I was doing.

"I'm writing a book," I said.

Of course, he replied as most children do to any statement made by their parents:

"WHY?"

I explained how I've had a unique opportunity to learn a lot about video and marketing, and that I wanted to share what I've learned with others. Only to realize that he wasn't asking me *why* I was writing the book, he was asking me why I was *writing* a book.

From his perspective, why wouldn't I be making a video, a podcast, or a voice-activated online service instead? Something people can *play* rather than read?

Point taken.

To be clear, it's not that my children don't read, or that they don't love a good storybook. However, when it comes to learning, sharing, and being entertained, their preferences are now voice and video.

During homework time, phrases like *"Hey Google, what's six times nine?"* or *"Let's search YouTube for that!"* are increasingly common.

Amelie, my soon-to-be "screenager," shares videos every day using Tik-Tok, Instagram, Snapchat, and a myriad of other apps that now include *record* and *play* buttons. Alec spends his weekends making iMovies with his friends. My four-year-old daughter, Juliette, turns on Netflix and finds the exact episode of Peppa Pig she wants to watch—all in a matter of *seconds*. My seven-year-old son, William, aspires to be a YouTuber. Not a firefighter or an engineer, but a YouTuber.

And when schools and businesses were closed due the coronavirus (COVID-19) pandemic, nearly all of their lessons and courseware shifted to online video, breeding a whole new generation of "ZOOMers" virtually overnight.

To them, video is simple, engaging, and expected. It's truly fascinating (and occasionally terrifying) to observe as a parent—and to consider as a business leader—how these new baseline expectations will impact how we connect with customers in the years ahead.

It's already started with video conferencing and two-minute explainers becoming the norm. However, this is only the beginning of the self-service visual age for business where video has a massive role to play.

While members of the "Millennial" and "Gen Z" generations have grown up during a time when video is highly accessible and immediate, the reality is that we're all hardwired to love video content, no matter our age.

In fact, according to Nielsen's 2018 Total Audience Report, the average adult in the United States now spends nearly six hours per day watching video across their television, laptop, smartphone, tablet, and TV-connected media devices.

Add to that the more than 1 billion hours of video consumed every day on YouTube, and you start to appreciate just how ingrained video has become in our daily lives.

And while video creation and publishing have traditionally been an expensive proposition for most businesses, we now carry high-definition video cameras in our pockets, and many business-grade video hosting services are free to get started.

The opportunity in front of you *right now* is to capitalize on the power of video in your business to attract more prospects, earn their trust, and deliver an exceptional customer experience—whether you're selling to millennials or boomers, business professionals or consumers.

To master the art of video in your own marketing and sales, it's important to understand *why* people have such a voracious appetite for it. And the secret to why we love video lies much deeper than our love of entertainment.

It lies in human biology and how our brains process different forms of information.

Chapter 2

THE POWER
OF VIDEO IS AS
EASY AS THE 4Es

Video is a fundamentally different medium than text and static content. It isn't just a different way to tell the same story; it's a *richer* way to tell a *bigger* story.

It's the perfect medium for explaining complex ideas, the most effective way to connect on an emotional level, and the next best thing to being there in person when it comes to establishing trust.

The key characteristics of video—and what makes it so powerful—can be easily remembered with what I call *the four Es of video*:

1. **Video is educational:** It's faster to process and easier to remember.
2. **Video is engaging:** It enables us to tell stories and hold audience attention.

3. **Video is emotional:** It can invoke joy, anticipation, trust and other emotions.

4. **Video shows empathy:** It helps us relate and connect on a human level.

Few will argue that these four Es are essential to attracting, converting, and retaining more buyers—and video is the ideal way to bring these to life.

VIDEO IS EDUCATIONAL

I live just outside of Toronto, Canada, and it's no secret that our winters can be a bit chilly.

And while I love the feel of the fresh cold air on a sunny winter's morn, I don't love the sound of my car attempting to start with a dying... dying... dead battery the morning after a deep freeze. I still remember when I had to jump-start my car for the very first time on a frozen winter morning.

Gloves off, hands freezing, anxious that I was going to electrocute myself *and* blow up my car, I still remember what I did that day. I pulled out my trusty BlackBerry and searched "how to jump-start a car." I then read the step-by-step instructions from two different online sources and felt fairly confident I could tackle this without doing any permanent damage.

"But wait," I thought to myself.

"What exactly does it mean when it says to connect it to the positive battery terminal? I think I know what the terminal is, but now I'm really regretting not taking auto shop classes in high school."

So, to be sure, I hopped over to YouTube and watched a short video of someone demonstrating exactly how to jump-start a car.

A *real* person with *real* jumper cables and real cars. And, most of all, *no explosions.*

Thanks to that video, I was able to clearly see how to accomplish the task without anything being lost in translation. To this day, I can still see it in my head, that video of my online savior connecting red, red, black, black, then hearing that engine hum.

The visual version of those instructions offered complete clarity, a high degree of trust, and a very memorable explanation in a way that simple words could not.

There are a number of reasons why video is the most effective and memorable way to learn about a new topic. According to recent studies, the human brain processes visual information 60,000 times faster than text-based information. That means we can learn more from watching a 60-second video than from reading text-based content for 10 minutes or more.

Think about what that means for your busy prospects and customers who have limited time to spare to learn about your solutions.

Humans also store visual information in long-term memory, rather than short-term memory—a critical factor in our survival as a species—while text is handled in short-term memory.

And, as illustrated in my own example, video affords you the opportunity to clearly see how something is done, what it looks like, or how to complete a process whether you're learning about jumper cables, home insurance, or the latest A.I. technology for your sales team.

VIDEO IS ENGAGING

Consider the power of great storytelling when brought to life on the big—or small—screen. Whether you cried during *Titanic*, cheered when *Harry Potter* defeated Voldemort, or simply *had* to see how things would play out in *Game of Thrones*, I'm sure you can recall countless times when you've gotten pulled right into a great story and felt compelled to keep watching.

So, it shouldn't come as a surprise that our brains are hardwired to engage in a storytelling narrative.

Research studies suggest that we're instinctively attracted to visual stories because they are how we have processed our most important information for millions of years. Stories are like healthy candy for our brains, so there's no need to feel guilty for binge-watching an entire season of *The Good Place* (if you haven't seen it, that's your homework this weekend).

People are also more likely to stay engaged with content that has a sense of movement and progression. A recent study by Facebook on "the persuasive power of video" found that people tend to gaze five times longer at videos in their social feeds compared to static text. Meanwhile on Instagram, a simple cinemagraph—a static image that moves ever so slightly—captures people's attention twice as long as a comparable static image.

Bottom line, if you're looking to draw people into your story and keep them engaged longer, look no further than video.

VIDEO IS EMOTIONAL

A few years back, The American Society for the Prevention of Cruelty to Animals released a powerful commercial featuring a montage of homeless cats and dogs with unbearably sad music playing in the background.

The ad was not only memorable, it was hugely successful for the ASPCA, which raised $30 million for the organization in the first two years of its release.

As the proud owner of the cutest little French bulldog you've ever seen, the video struck a particularly strong chord for me, in addition to hitting home with thousands (if not millions) of others.

The success of the ASPCA's campaign can undoubtedly be attributed to its evocation of emotion in viewers, and how it got them invested in the outcome of this story. Even if your business isn't saving lives or rescuing animals, there are countless ways to tap into your audience's emotions through creative storytelling.

Decades of research have shown how emotion influences human decision-making in a major way and ignites audiences to take action. If sadness doesn't suit your brand, consider playing on humor, joy, trust, anticipation, or surprise as ways to stimulate an emotional connection.

Adobe's "Mean Streets" video—in which a desperate CMO goes searching for clicks in all the wrong places (think dark alleyways and suspicious characters selling fake *likes* and *views*)—is a hilarious, on-point example of how effective humor can be when done right, especially in B2B where audiences aren't expecting it.

VIDEO SHOWS EMPATHY

Terminus, a leading provider of account-based marketing software solutions, recently experimented with personalized video messages as part of their enterprise sales process.

In addition to their typical email and phone outreach, sales reps began recording short videos using their webcams as a way to introduce themselves to new prospects. The videos provided an opportunity to connect as real people and to prove, using visuals and their own body language, that they understood the problems their prospects were facing.

Not only did they see a whopping 300% increase in response rates, they also found prospects were responding in a much more casual and personal tone. On top of that, the number of meetings booked went up, while no-shows and cancellations went down. Much of that success was

To help you, we'll breakdown the fundamental elements of becoming a media company and show exactly how you can create a culture of video in-house.

Yes, you read that correctly—**in-house**.

After all, you are a media company, aren't you?

OK, so now that we've covered the "why" of video and what makes it so powerful, let's get to the meat and potatoes.

To start, I'm going to discuss how sales teams can use video in their everyday sales process, and then Tyler will do a deep-dive into how marketing teams can powerfully integrate video into every facet of their job.

THE ART OF VIDEO FOR SALES

A Note from Marcus Sheridan

I used to be a pool guy.

"Wait a minute, what does a pool guy know about video?"

That's a valid question—but before you dismiss what you're about to read, I want to ask you to hang in there for at least a few pages.

You see, for years, my job was cut and dry.

In-ground swimming pool shoppers would call our company, River Pools and Spas. Then, in most cases, I would make the long drive to their home with the intention to, yes, sell them a swimming pool.

More often than not, when I would knock on the door of a home for one of these sales calls, I'd hear a child's voice in the background yell out something to the effect of, "Mom, Dad, the pool guy is here!"

(When a family is considering an in-ground swimming pool in their backyard, you can rest assured the children know that the "pool guy" is coming over. It's like Santa Claus was coming to town.)

So, that was me. Just a pool guy. No name. No face.

Just a knock on the door.

But then, one night, after we had embraced the philosophy of what I now call "The Visual Sale," everything changed.

You see, on that particular occasion, as I knocked on the door, I heard a child in the background say, "Mom, Dad, **the guy on the video** is here!"

An eyebrow immediately raised.

The child knew **my face.**

I wasn't just another pool guy. I was more than that. *Much more.*

But the story doesn't stop there.

A year or so later, at the end of my career as a swimming pool sales guy—I still own the company today as a silent partner—I had another occasion when I walked up to a front door for a sales appointment and something absolutely magical happened.

"Mom, Dad, *Marcus* from the video is here."

I had a name. I had a face. They knew me.

Think that sales appointment was just like any other?

Oh no, not at all.

We didn't need to spend the majority of our time together establishing our relationship and building trust. They already knew who I was, so we were already way past that.

Everything was faster.

Everything was better.

Everything was more effective.

So much so that the family bought a pool. That night. No hesitation. No need for "just a few more quotes." We were already where we needed to be, without the need for additional hand-holding or steps—all thanks to my proactive use of video in the sales process.

It was because of this experience my eyes were opened to a definitive reality:

 The Visual Sale is real.

Chapter 4

6 VIDEOS THAT WILL IMMEDIATELY IMPACT SALES AND CLOSING RATES

As we've already stated, inducing trust is at the core of using any form of video as a business. But once you move past trust and pose the question of *"Why video?"* the answer should always start with sales, not marketing.

That's right. Video is a sales initiative.

Whether you're B2B, B2C, service, product, e-commerce, etc., your goal is to induce enough trust to make more sales for your organization.

This is why your sales team should feel as if almost every video you create as an organization is another tool in their toolbox that will lead them closer to their goals. The fact is, they should be thrilled when they hear another video has been produced by the company's video or marketing team.

But sadly, too often when companies produce video content, they don't focus on the stuff that actually generates the greatest return on investment (ROI) and trust. As a result, the sales team often believes those videos are "marketing fluff," offering little to no usefulness in the sales process.

For example, the number one video we see most companies invest in and create first is the "about us" video.

Yes, "about us" videos may be nice, but when was the last time your sales team said:

"I can't wait to start using our new 'about us' video in my sales pitch!"

Likely never.

What they're looking for, as you know, is content that will overcome prospect concerns, address common fears, and clearly answer buyer questions.

Later on in the book, Tyler will discuss marketing videos that align with every phase of the traditional buyer's funnel. But when it comes to helping your sales team, unlike the many marketing videos you'll soon read about, we always want to focus on the *bottom* of the funnel first. In other words, what do buyers really want to know?

Furthermore, if your organization is going to invest time, effort, and resources into video production, then eventually your CFO, controller, or accountant is going to ask a critical question:

"Is this video stuff actually making us any money?"

If the answer is "no" or "I'm not sure," then we have a serious problem.

"About us" videos are the ultimate "I'm not sure."

Even the best intentions in business will eventually be cut-off or eliminated if their value is not proven. This is why, ideally, your sales team should be saying, "I couldn't come close to being as effective as I am if we weren't producing this video content."

Additionally, your prospects should be raving to you about how helpful your videos were during the research process.

If this isn't happening, again, we have a problem.

Let's say we agree that videos should be created to help the sales team right now, and we're ready to get started. What comes next?

Well, that's where the following list of videos for sales came into play. These were created over the course of a few years (and a few hundred B2C and B2B client case studies) with our team at IMPACT.

Because we were in uncharted waters with these clients in teaching them in-house video, we knew most would need to see quick results. Otherwise, and understandably so, they would pull the plug.

Thus, we knew the videos would have to generate immediate revenue, i.e. sell.

Once you read about each of these, your initial reaction will very likely be, "OK, this is a no-brainer. Why aren't we already doing this?"

But, as is often the case in business, we overcomplicate very simple truths.

Chapter 5

THE 80% VIDEO

If you talk to most sales teams and ask them what percentage of the questions they get on a sales call are exactly the same from call to call, the vast majority will give you a number between 70% and 90%.

That's because sales teams answer the same questions over and over again, day in and day out. And it can get pretty old.

Ask any sales professional, "What are the questions you are commonly asked that tell you a prospect is clearly not ready to buy?"

They will recite an extensive catalog of those questions as an answer.

Anyone who has been in sales for any period of time understands this all too well.

But what would happen if, every time you had a sales call, not only did your prospect already know the answer to those all-too-common questions, but they had seen it, heard it, and learned it from you?

Yep, the sales appointment would be dramatically more productive.

And not just more productive, but much shorter, too.

Now, instead of spending so much time answering those universal questions, you can focus your conversation around addressing your prospect's very specific questions that are unique to their needs and circumstances.

You also wouldn't have to spend nearly as much time building relationships of trust on the front-end of the appointment because it will have already been established long before you shake the prospect's hand.

This is exactly why the 80% video is so imperative for sales success.

PUTTING IT INTO ACTION

The 80% video process is simple:

- Brainstorm a list of the most important products and/or services your company offers. Eventually, you will create an 80% video for each.

- Have your sales team (or anyone that deals with a prospect) brainstorm the most common questions they get on a typical sales call regarding that particular product or service. At a minimum, you should be able to come up with 10 questions.

- Once you've completed your brainstorm, narrow your list down to the top seven questions. These will constitute your core 80%. (If you're wondering whether or not you can choose more or less than seven, the answer is yes. We've simply found with our own clients that seven tends to be the most effective number.)

- Answer each question in an individual video. This video can— and generally should be—uploaded to your company's YouTube page and utilized anywhere else that is potentially helpful to buyers on your website.

- Take these seven videos and combine them into one long video. This will be your 80% video.

- Immediately get this video in the hands of your sales team and integrate it into the sales process, with the core purpose being that of having prospects view it before the initial appointment.

As you might imagine, the 80% video is incredibly effective, when done properly. Chances are, however, if you're like most clients or audiences we speak to, you likely have some questions at this point.

Because this video is so monumentally important to your business going forward, we're going to take some time here to thoroughly cover the questions you're going to run into once you start producing this type of video.

Please do not skim this section.

Your understanding of these seemingly "inconsequential" details will be the difference between achieving massive success and experiencing pitiful results.

COMMON QUESTIONS REGARDING THE 80% VIDEO

1. How long should the 80% video be? Aren't you afraid the prospect won't watch something that is long?

One of the most ridiculous statistics in the history of the internet is the idea that "all videos should be short" or that "all videos should be less than 90 seconds."

Yes, it is true that when a video extends beyond 90 seconds, the watch rates dip. But the same is true after the first three seconds of watching a video. But does that mean all videos should be three seconds? *Of course not.*

Our philosophy at IMPACT (and shared by Tyler and his team at Vidyard), one that has worked incredibly well for hundreds of clients, is simple:

Answer the question as concisely, yet thoroughly, as possible.

Yes, you read that correctly.

We want them to be concise in the way they communicate—to the point, clear, and incisive. But we also want them to be thorough enough to empower the prospect or buyer to say by the end of it, "Perfect. Now I understand."

By adhering to this philosophy, you won't have to spend so much time debating the frustrating question, "How long should this video be?" Instead, you can start getting to work.

When it comes to the optimal length of a video, far and away, the most significant factor is where the buyer is in the sales cycle.

For example, if you just started thinking about buying a swimming pool last night, you likely only want to watch short videos or read shorter content on the subject.

But, if you know that a salesperson is coming to your house tomorrow and that you might sign a contract for $50,000 to $100,000 for a swimming pool, there is a very, very good chance you'd be more than interested in watching a longer video.

In fact, our average customer at River Pools has watched more than 20 minutes of River Pools-produced video before they buy.

We've seen this trend with buyer watch-time replicated in many other industries as well, and it's not just about price alone. What's more, price isn't even the variable that best dictates how much video someone is willing to watch.

Rather, it comes down to this:

How great is their fear of making the wrong decision?

When we're afraid to make a wrong decision, we will spend as much time as it takes to get comfortable with our buying choices. This is the reality of the digital age.

2. Should one person or multiple people act as subject matter experts in an 80% video?

The primary goal for any video you produce is that communication is clear, effective, and helpful. If this means that you need to choose the one person on staff that is capable of this, then, by all means, get it done with that one person.

That being said, in a perfect world, it often comes across as very impressive to the viewer when multiple subject matter experts from your company play a part in these videos.

Again, it's not a must, but it does make a difference.

You'll also find that some salespeople want to create their own 80% video for prospects. This certainly makes sense—at least in terms of their relationship with the prospect—and, as long as the quality meets your company's brand standards, then it's likely a good thing.

It also sets an example to the rest of the sales team that one of their peers is going above and beyond to build trust as quickly and as strongly as possible in the relationship.

3. What if we offer hundreds (if not thousands) of products or services? Do we have to create a video for each?

Obviously, it's unlikely that you're going to be able to create hundreds of 80% videos if your company sells hundreds of products. Of course, if you do have multiple products and services that you offer, ask yourself these two questions:

- What are the 20% of products and/or services that we sell that generate 80% of the revenue? (Pareto's Law)
- What are the products and/or services that have the greatest untapped potential and opportunity for our organization?

Just by answering these two questions, you'll now have a strong sense as to which products and services need to come first.

4. What should a salesperson say to ensure that more prospects actually watch the video before a sales appointment?

Most sales teams still struggle with properly using content (be it text, video, podcasts, and so on) in the sales process. For example, they often invite prospects to watch video using incredibly weak language, as demonstrated in the following:

"We have some excellent videos on our website. It would be great if you could watch a few of them before our next meeting."

That's not effective. It's a passive suggestion.

Instead, here is an ideal script that your sales team can follow:

> **Salesperson:** *Mr. Jones, I know it's important to you that when we meet to discuss (product/service) that we don't waste any of your time. Not only that, I'm sure it's safe to say you don't want to make any mistakes along the way.*
>
> *As to ensure you don't make any of the common mistakes we see buyers make, we've created a video that addresses the top seven questions and concerns people just like you have when making this type of decision.*
>
> *By watching this video, you'll save time, money, and eliminate the stress of potential buying mistakes. Plus, our time together will be dramatically more productive and effective.*
>
> *Will you take the time to watch this video before our meeting on Friday?*

In the above sample script, the salesperson clearly states the value of the video in terms that lead with the needs and desires of the buyer. Moreover, the call-to-action is direct and time-bound.

5. Can this video be used in customer service?

Not only can you use 80% videos within your customer service department, but you absolutely should use them. Using video to quickly show customers how to fix or solve their customer service issues can save thousands upon thousands of dollars per year in unnecessary expenses.

To do this, find the most common (80%) customer service issues you're having with the major products and services that you offer. Then use these videos as part of your "purchase package" when onboarding new customers.

6. How does this type of video apply to e-commerce, when there is no "salesperson" involved?

Sadly, many companies believe that because they're e-commerce, the 80% video concept doesn't apply to them.

This couldn't be further from the truth.

In a perfect world, every major product you sell in e-commerce has an 80% video that is shown right there with it, readily available to shoppers to watch and resolve their most pressing questions and concerns.

7. Should these videos just be a "talking head" style, or does there have to be more production value?

Always remember, "some" is better than "none" when it comes to educational videos. In other words, a basic talking head video is much more effective than a robust, production-driven video that has never been published because it's lost in production purgatory.

That being said, over time, you will want to make improvements to your 80% video, especially when using b-roll (shots of the product or service, or even your people), so as to make it more visually clear whatever it is you're trying to explain to the viewer.

But don't be afraid to start basic and allow organic progress and growth from there.

8. What are the most common mistakes companies make with the 80% video?

As you may have gathered from other areas of this book, the biggest mistake companies make with their 80% video is that they overcomplicate the process. Typically, this occurs when they're too busy thinking like a business and not nearly busy enough thinking like an actual buyer.

(The same rule holds true for the rest of the videos listed herein.)

Great communication, in any video, but especially in the 80% video, has a tone that sounds something like:

> *"If you're considering _____, we know you have questions. You may even have concerns. But you can stop worrying because that's why we created this video. We want you to be informed. We also want you to be relaxed. So, let's address these concerns—and by the end of this video, you'll likely have a much better understanding of the questions that have been on your mind . . ."*

In conjunction with this, the other major mistake companies make is that they don't state questions as the buyer would. Rather, they state them as they, the business, would. Let's look at a quick example if you were selling a swimming pool.

Bad: "Why getting a diving board is a bad idea."

Good: "Is getting a diving board right for me and my family?"

Notice, the first one is biased, with a clearly stated opinion. The second is open and unbiased, written exactly as a potential buyer would articulate the question themselves if they were debating on a diving board for their swimming pool.

9. Can the 80% video be used throughout the sales process, not just before the first appointment?

Yes! One of the greatest benefits of this video type is its ability to influence other decision-makers who aren't present for actual sales conversations.

So often, sales are lost because the "messenger"—the individual who actually spoke with the salesperson—is unable to explain to the rest of the decision-makers the value of the product or service, or address their core questions regarding the product.

You see this a lot in the sales world.

For example, let's say one spouse was physically present for a sales appointment but the other wasn't able to attend.

When this occurs, often the spouse who was in attendance is left explaining (and therefore selling) to the other spouse the product's features, benefits, value proposition, and so on.

As you can well imagine, this is a salesperson's worst nightmare and is one of the biggest reasons why an apparent "hot lead" can go cold so quickly.

Leveraged properly, the 80% video absolutely can and should fill this void.

Chapter 6

EMPLOYEE BIO VIDEOS FOR EMAIL SIGNATURES

At its core, video, when done correctly, will humanize your business in a powerful way.

In a perfect world—where you are using video so well—potential customers and buyers are able to see, hear, and know you and your fellow employees before the first handshake ever occurs.

One of the best and simplest ways to do this is by creating what we refer to as a "bio" video for each one of your sales team members (or any others that are customer-facing for that matter).

A bio video accomplishes two goals:

- It explains what the person does for the company and why they chose this profession.
- It also gives a little bit of personal information about what they do when they're not at work.

By mixing a bit of personal and professional in a short video—typically, 90 to 120 seconds long—you now have the ability to visually introduce yourself much earlier in the sales process.

Although this video can be used in a variety of ways, such as on your "team" or "about us" pages of your company website, we have found that, by far, the most effective place for this video to be utilized is in **your email signature**.

Email signatures are dramatically underused and under-appreciated areas of digital real estate, especially as a sales and marketing tool. But when properly taken advantage of, their benefits can be significant.

If you were to look at a typical email signature, most people have the basics—name, company, contact information, social media profiles, and possibly an image of their face.

By also placing a bio video in this signature—with a clear thumbnail image denoting it's a video—you've now given your email recipients a chance to get to know you on a much more visual, and therefore human, level.

As we've helped implement these simple videos with sales teams around the world, we've consistently found an average of 25 to 30 additional views per month of the video when integrating it into an email signature.

Think about that for a second—that's 25 to 30 more people who now know your name, your face, your voice, and your story.

We've all heard a million times that we "buy from those we know, like, and trust."

Bio videos, when used properly, can help you drastically increase your odds of closing a deal by fostering closer connections between you and your prospects.

*(Want to see what a proper email signature with video looks like? Email me at **marcus@marcussheridan.com** and I'll respond with mine.)*

COMMON QUESTIONS REGARDING EMPLOYEE BIO VIDEOS

1. Who should be required within a company to have a bio video? What types of employees or positions?

Usually, we suggest to clients that they require each of their sales team members to have a bio video. Because relationship-building is such a critical part of sales, this only makes sense. Anyone else who is customer-facing, or is a member of your leadership team, should strongly consider utilizing a bio video as well.

2. Where else can bio videos reside?

Other than email signatures, the best place for this type of video to exist is on the "about us" or "team" pages of your website. In fact, in certain industries—for instance, medicine or healthcare—the "meet the team" page is often one of the most viewed pages of the website.

Beyond this, employees can and should integrate this video into their social media channels, especially LinkedIn.

3. Can employees produce these themselves, on their phones, or does there need to be more of a production element involved?

As always in this book, Tyler and I advocate that attempting to do (and learn) video is a good thing for any organization and its employees, regardless of how simple or basic the videos may be. That being said, if you have a choice to make the videos look and feel more professional, then, of course, you should.

Just don't let this quest for perfection hinder your ability to get started.

Chapter 7

PRODUCT AND SERVICE FIT VIDEOS

When it comes to the traffic on most organization's websites, "product" or "service" pages are (usually) the most trafficked.

The way these pages are designed, at least from a messaging stand-point, is often extremely flawed. Why? Because all these pages tend to espouse why their product or service is great, what it is, what it does, etc.

But for those businesses that understand the way buyers actually think, there is an essential second part to the type of information this page must include, and that is simply this:

*Who is the product or service **not** for?*

Yes, you read that correctly—not for.

Now, you may be wondering why.

Well, the minute we are willing (as businesses) to say what we're not is the precise moment we become dramatically more attractive to those for whom we are a good fit.

Therein lies the key to a product or service fit video. It explains who the product is—and is not—a good fit for in the most honest and transparent way possible.

COMMON QUESTIONS REGARDING PRODUCT AND SERVICE FIT VIDEOS

1. Can it be used in other applications other than product or service pages?

Yes! That's the beauty of these videos. Their most effective use cases are often found by sales teams as they leverage them throughout different stages of the sales process.

2. How long should a fit video be?

Unlike the 80% video, which addresses multiple questions, a product or service fit video is really only addressing two—who or what is a good fit, and who or what is a bad fit? Therefore, in most cases, this video will be shorter than five minutes. As is always the case, this number will vary drastically depending on the complexity of the answer.

3. What are the biggest mistakes companies make with a fit video?

The biggest issue we've seen with clients upon implementing fit videos has to do with the tone in which the subject matter expert delivers the message. To help you understand what I mean by tone, let's look at two examples—one good and one bad—referencing a fiberglass swimming pool.

Good: *"You may be asking yourself, 'is a fiberglass pool a good fit for me?'*
Great question, and it's an important one too, as this is the type of deci-
sion you won't be able to go back on once it's in the ground. Like any type
of swimming pool, fiberglass comes with a set of pros and cons.

For example, because the pool shells don't get wider than 16 feet or longer
than 40 feet, there are clear size restrictions. Also, because the manu-
facturing process includes pre-designed "molds" to build the pool off of,
you can't customize a pool's shape, size, depth, etc., beyond what you see
within our available models.

But, if you're looking for a low-maintenance pool that's smaller than
16-by-40 feet, less than 8 feet deep—and you are able to find a shape
that fits your needs—fiberglass might be a great fit for you."

Bad: *"You may be asking, 'Why should I consider a fiberglass pool.' Well,*
the reasons are obvious. They are way less maintenance, you won't have
to replaster them or replace the liner, and they go in way faster than any
other type of swimming pool.

But if you don't care about cleaning your pool all day long and want the
added burdens that come with other types of swimming pools, fiberglass
may not be the best fit for you."

Hopefully, you can see the obvious differences in the content, tone, and
style of these two examples.

As we've stressed many times in this book, everything comes down
to trust. If it will induce more trust (because it's true), then you're on the
right track. But if the tone doesn't do this (due to arrogance, dishonesty,
or omission), then it's clearly not good for the business or the customer.

Chapter 8

COST AND
PRICING VIDEOS

Remember, the primary purpose of embracing a culture of video is to move the needle for the sales team, which is why we must keep this in mind when considering the question, "Should we discuss cost and price on our website and content?"

Well, the answer—especially if you read *They Ask, You Answer*—is a huge "Yes!" And although we can't go into all the psychological reasons as to why we should be willing to discuss this subject, consider this:

How many times a month does your sales team justify why something costs what it costs?

The thing is, consumers and buyers are researching this question of "cost" prolifically, and unless someone explains to them how to define "value" on the front end (before they talk to a salesperson), then ignorance will prevail. And when ignorance prevails, price wars and commoditization are the only results.

To combat this, we need to be willing to discuss (and teach about) cost, price, rates, etc. And to do this the right way, a video on cost and pricing should:

- Address all the factors that drive the cost of a product or service up or down.

- Discuss the marketplace—i.e., why are comparable products or services cheap, expensive, etc.?

- Talk about your product or service, and why it costs what it costs. *(Although you don't have to give your exact pricing here, you do need to explain your value proposition extremely well while giving the buyer at least a sense for what to expect.)*

As we discussed previously, one of the great benefits of using video in the sales process is its ability to overcome communication gaps that occur when a salesperson isn't able to fully discuss a product or service with all decision-makers.

Now, instead of the "messenger" explaining to the other decision-makers what he or she heard when meeting with the salesperson, this video can and should justify the overall value of the product way better than another person could.

COMMON QUESTIONS REGARDING COST AND PRICING VIDEOS

1. Wouldn't "how much does it cost" just go into the 80% video?

You can certainly address how much something costs in an 80% video, but time and time again, we've found with clients that, because understanding cost is such a pivotal part of the buying process, it merits its own attention.

By producing a singular video that dives deep into cost, value, factors, etc., you can powerfully educate a buyer and induce a tremendous amount of trust in the process. Plus, by being an individual piece of content that is very specific, it has a greater chance of doing well in search, social, etc.

2. How long should a cost video be?

Of all the sales videos mentioned herein, this one will vary the most when it comes to length. We've helped clients produce incredibly effective cost videos that were less than two minutes, while others were longer than 10 minutes. Again, concisely answer the question as thoroughly as possible.

3. How specific should a cost video be?

We have found that specificity with cost and price is almost always a good thing. For example, in the past, manufacturers wouldn't ever mention pricing because, in their minds, it would upset potential retailers or distributors.

But times have changed, which is exactly why more and more manufacturers are at least including the manufacturer's suggested retail price (MSRP) on their website as that sets some sort of realistic expectation for the end buyer.

Having experimented with this with dozens and dozens of our clients at IMPACT, I can tell you that, almost always, the more specific a company is willing to be in answering questions about cost and pricing, the greater the increase in trust, leads, and ultimately revenue.

4. How many cost videos should a company create?

For every major product or service that you sell, you want to have at least one video that specifically teaches the components of cost, price, and value.

"But what if we sell hundreds of products and services?"

If that's the case, start with the products or services that have (or could potentially have) the greatest impact on your company's bottom line. Then work your way down from there.

Chapter 9

CUSTOMER JOURNEY VIDEOS

At this point in the digital age, most companies have at least some type of "social proof" on their website, including customer quotes, testimonials, written case studies, and so on. Although these are helpful and relevant in earning buyer trust, none compare to a true "customer journey video."

We call it the customer journey video because the idea is that it's designed to follow the principle of the "hero's journey"—something that movie producers and storytellers (like Disney) have used since the beginning of time.

Now, the traditional hero's journey has 12 parts. In the context of your customers, however, this journey can be simplified into three main stages:

Stage 1: Your customer has a problem—a need, stress, worry, concern, or issue.

Stage 2: The journey they take to fix their problem. (In most cases, this is the journey they go on with your company.)

Stage 3: Where they are today and how they were able to fix the problem with your help. (And everyone lived happily ever after.)

At its core, the purpose of this video is that a viewer can watch it and literally say in their mind:

"They're just like me. They had the exact problem I have right now, and look at how they were able to solve it."

In other words, your viewer is literally "nodding along" in affirmation because of sympathy, empathy, and mutual understanding.

Of course, you may read this and say, "Duh, Marcus. This is common sense."

The reality, however, is most companies have not produced videos like this. Fact is, the companies that do are few and far between, mainly because organizations haven't thought about them or decided they would be too difficult to get customers to agree to.

But it's our experience that, in most industries, many customers are absolutely willing to do a video like this for a business assuming that business did a great job solving their problem or addressing their needs, which makes the recording process as simple and friction-free as possible.

Once again, the key to the success of these videos is the intentional integration of them by the sales team in the sales process. In fact, I've personally had more than one occasion when a prospect was on the fence and by simply watching a customer journey video (that they could relate to) they then decided to move forward with the agreement.

Once again, this is the beauty of the visual sale.

Note: You should always get written permission from customers when using them in your videos.

Chapter 10

"CLAIMS WE MAKE" VIDEOS

Every business likes to make claims about itself. And sales professionals, when pitching to potential customers, will often make the same claims. For example:

"We are the best_____."

"We have the most _____."

"No one does _____ like we do."

Your own list of claims probably goes on and on.

When it comes to these claims we make, we generally take our clients through a powerful exercise:

- Brainstorm the claims you make as a company. (Typically, you'll find them on your website, in your sales messaging, etc.)

- Next, ask yourself, "How many of our competitors make a similar, if not the same, claim as the ones we have listed?"

- Finally, ask yourself, "How many of these claims have we visually proven (through video) and not just stated?"

The activity is simple, yet it's eye-opening.

Most industry "claims" are repeated over and over by the competing businesses therein. And if everyone is stating the same claims, what do they actually mean to the marketplace?

Yep, claims such as these are just noise… until someone shows them to be true. You do just that with a "claims we make" video.

Let's look at a specific example.

One of the most popular claims businesses make around the world is, "It's our people that make us different."

Fine, fair enough. ***Your people are different.***

But what makes that true? How am I supposed to know?

In other words, to truly prove such a claim, you must show your people—their stories, their background, how they got where they are, and so on. By doing so, others will inevitably say, "Wow, their people really are different."

COMMON QUESTIONS REGARDING "CLAIMS WE MAKE" VIDEOS

1. What's the difference between a "claims we make" video and an "about us" video?

In an ideal world, an "about us" video, done the right way, will do exactly what a "claims we make" video does—it will visually prove what makes your company unique, special, and different.

It will take viewers behind the scenes and allow them to get to know you on a level that makes them intuit something more genuine regarding your organization than the others they've looked at and dealt with.

49

That being said, most "about us" videos aren't done this way, and therefore end up being a waste of time and money, as mentioned earlier in this chapter.

2. What if you don't have anything that makes you unique?

There is so much fundamentally wrong with this question, but it's one we hear often. If you're asking about this for your company, it's important to understand a couple of things:

- Just by you being willing to "show it"—whatever "it" is—makes you special, different, and unique.

- As businesses, because we're so entrenched in what we do, we tend to devalue the uniqueness of our product or service. Remember, if someone is buying it, it is interesting.

So, there you have it, six videos absolutely designed to be used by your sales team to close more deals.

As you can see, there are actually more than six total videos here, as each type leads to potentially multiple visual opportunities to teach, show, and sell. In fact, if you have a full-time videographer, there's a good chance these videos will require at least a year's worth of work.

Don't let this intimidate you.

They're an amazing opportunity for the sales team when used properly. Just remember to stay away from the fluff. Address what buyers really want to know and trust will always follow.

PART III

THE EVOLUTION OF BUYER BEHAVIOR AND MARKETING

Chapter 11

THE MOST COMMON MARKETING CHALLENGES

When I first joined Vidyard in 2014, I underestimated how much I would learn as a marketing leader in a business that sits at the intersection of marketing technology and creative content.

Not only has it been a forcing function to stay on top of the latest marketing trends, but it's provided an opportunity to see how other businesses are tackling these two areas in tandem, and how their priorities are shifting.

While I've learned that every business has its own unique set of marketing challenges, a few consistent themes have stood out across *all* of my conversations with marketers:

1. Priorities Are a Moving Target

The priorities of marketing teams continue to shift from 'outbound' paid sponsorships and advertising to 'inbound' content marketing, search engine marketing, and social media.

2. Digital Channel Expansion and Diversification

The digital channels being used to reach prospects are continuing to diversify, with marketers now embracing search engine marketing, website optimization, email, social media, blogs, YouTube, Instagram, review sites, chatbots, and more.

3. Increased Responsibility

Marketers have a greater responsibility than ever before for generating results throughout the entire customer lifecycle—from lead generation and deal acceleration, to post-sale customer marketing—leading to a "full-funnel" marketing mentality.

4. Offline Goes Online

Accelerated even further by the COVID-19 pandemic, businesses are embracing an online-first mentality across marketing, sales, and customer service. Virtual events, virtual meetings, and online digital experiences are now the preferred and (often) only way to deliver programs.

What's interesting to note is that these common challenges all seem to stem from one primary root cause: *the changing behaviors and expectations of today's buyers.*

Chapter 12

NEW BUYER BEHAVIORS LEAD TO A NEW WORLD OF MARKETING

Once upon a time, our buyers consumed traditional advertisements (television, radio, magazine, and so on) as a way to learn about products and services. They contacted a small number of vendors with whom they were familiar early on in their discovery process to learn about capabilities and pricing.

Sales reps were invited onsite to meet their team and provide a live demonstration. There may have even been a golf game in the mix.

This led to marketers being more focused on advertising and brand awareness, while sales reps focused on education, relationship building, qualification, and closing.

Today's buyers, on the other hand, have immediate access to an infinite pool of online content, connections, reviews, and followers, and are much less inclined to follow the buyer's journey of yore.

In fact, Sirius Decisions and Forrester Research, two leading research and analysis firms in marketing and sales strategy, have both reported that more than 80% of the buyer's journey now happens online in a self-service fashion, before they even think about contacting a vendor directly or speaking with someone in sales.

And that was *before* the "great virtualization" we saw as a result of the COVID-19 pandemic.

So, what does this mean for today's marketer? **A heck of a lot.**

Now, your team is not only responsible for brand awareness and lead generation, but also for educating audiences through the buying process, maximizing online engagement, building memorable relationships, and doing it all at scale through digital content.

Marketing has become the *sales rep that never sleeps*, and every marketer needs to think more like a seller as they become responsible for an expanding part of the buyer's journey.

This is something I live and breathe every day at Vidyard, where our team measures success not just on website traffic and new leads, but also on the amount of pipeline and revenue we're helping the business generate. This has a big impact on the channels and programs we focus on, the type of content we create, and the role that video plays throughout the new buyer's journey.

Chapter 13

THE BUYER'S JOURNEY, THE ROLE OF MARKETING, AND WHAT IT MEANS FOR VIDEO

The buyer's journey, according to HubSpot, is "the process buyers go through to become aware of, consider and evaluate, and decide to purchase a new product or service."

While there is no single representation of this journey that can be applied to *every* type of product or service, a commonly used model breaks it down into the following four stages:

1. Awareness: The potential buyer gains awareness of a brand, product, or service, the problems it can solve, and the benefits it can offer. Common channels for gaining awareness include online search, social media, blogs and content, advertisements, direct mail, webinars, word-of-mouth, influencers, analyst reports, trade shows, and more.

2. Consideration: The buyer educates themselves further on potential solutions and vendors. Common channels include online search, vendor websites, third party review sites, blogs, email marketing, direct conversations with sales reps, and educational resources such as videos, e-books, and webinars.

3. Decision: The buyer has narrowed down the potential solutions, secured budget, and is preparing to make a buying decision. This stage is often managed by a sales rep and is supported by content provided by marketing such as customer testimonials, competitive comparisons, and on-demand demonstrations.

4. Post-sale retention, upsell, and referral: While most marketers have traditionally focused on pre-sale stages of the buyer's journey, more emphasis is being placed on this stage as social media, peer review sites, and referrals become a bigger part of how today's prospects evaluate solutions. Or, more simply, marketing now plays a critical role in customer satisfaction and customer advocacy as a means of generating new sales opportunities.

Marketers are no longer just responsible for generating brand awareness and running the company website. They need to think carefully about each stage of the buyer's journey.

Because video is such a flexible content medium, it can not only be used throughout the buyer's journey, but also across virtually every marketing program and channel that you may invest in today.

For the remainder of the following three parts of this book, we'll explore the types of videos you can use at each stage of the buyer's journey and how those videos align with the most common marketing programs and channels.

I've organized the content in this way to make it easier to appreciate how video can be incorporated into your *existing* marketing efforts. You can also share different chapters of this book with others who may be responsible for specific marketing programs or channels.

But first, I've got an inspiring story to share about a rapidly growing business using video throughout the buyer's journey to transform the narrative—and their results—in a highly competitive market.

Chapter 14

MIOVISION TRANSFORMS EVERY STEP OF THE BUYER'S JOURNEY IN A NOTORIOUSLY SLOW-MOVING INDUSTRY

"Video scares a lot of marketers. They think they need a full-time videographer on staff or an expensive outside agency. But after I got my digital camera and we enabled our account team with a webcam recording tool, we just started making videos! The feedback has been terrific and we're seeing some amazing results."

Matt Trushinski, Director of Marketing, Miovision

Your business may have it tough.

You might be in a slow-moving market where prospects don't seem to respond to traditional marketing and sales tactics. Maybe you're a relatively unknown brand competing with large established incumbents. Or perhaps you think that your audience won't engage with social media, chatbots, or online video because that's *just not how your industry works*.

If any of these perceived challenges sound familiar, rest assured that the team at Miovision can relate. Founded 12 years ago as a provider of traffic data information services to regional municipalities, Miovision sells into a traditional industry that is notoriously slow-moving.

VIEWING CHALLENGES AS OPPORTUNITIES

Miovision's competitors are established transportation companies and data providers, many of which have been around for decades, with long-standing relationships throughout their market. And one might assume that back-office government employees prefer whitepapers, PDFs, and emails over rich media, making it difficult to earn their attention with modern visual content.

But instead of letting these challenges stand in their way, Miovision flipped them on their head, embracing them as *opportunities to stand out and differentiate* within a crowded legacy market.

In fact, Matt Trushinski, director of marketing at Miovision, sees their small size and modern approach to marketing as key advantages over larger competitors.

As a smaller business, they tend to be more creative, experimental, and agile. They've built their marketing engine on a modern technology stack that enables them to engage audiences through various content mediums on multiple channels. And, soon after they began experimenting with video content, they proved something that may seem obvious in hindsight, but is often easy to forget:

Their prospects aren't just government employees; they're real people who see value in educational, emotional, and engaging visual content.

VIDEO WAS NO ONE-TRICK PONY

Matt began injecting video into Miovision's marketing programs shortly after purchasing a basic digital camera and tripod. His initial efforts focused on thought leadership to build their brand and clearly explain the unique value they offer.

In parallel to his own efforts, he found that one of his colleagues in customer support was also creating videos using do-it-yourself screen capture and webcam recording tools. More people started getting on board and video soon became a key part of how they engaged both prospects and customers.

Purpose-built videos are now used to boost engagement on their website, expand their audience on social media, increase conversion rates on email campaigns, and more. They're even using short videos to promote new product launches, events, and upcoming webinars:

> *"Every time we go to execute on a process we ask ourselves, 'What are the stages where we can leverage video?' For instance, as soon as we have a topic for a webinar, we now book a filming date and in one sitting record a webinar invitation video, a date reminder video, a 'thanks for coming' follow up video, and a 'sorry we missed you' video.*
>
> *No matter what path a prospect might take, we have a piece of video content custom-tailored for that purpose. We also record the webinar and cut it up into chunks. This way, at every step of the marketing and sales process, our prospects have video of someone talking them through it.*

It not only helps to drive greater engagement, but it builds an ongoing relationship with the real people at Miovision."

Matt Trushinski, Director of Marketing, Miovision

THE NUMEROUS BENEFITS OF VIDEO FOR MIOVISION

Video has helped Miovision stand out from its competition and create brand recognition. It's also driving familiarity with sales prospects by putting faces to names. Through video, a prospect may hear from a product marketing manager they met at a tradeshow, meet the sales rep who is responsible for their account, or regularly interact with other "faces" of the Miovision brand.

These videos are all created in-house with nothing more than a webcam or a basic digital camera. The biggest obstacle wasn't the technology or budget, but rather having the discipline and courage to start capturing content in creative new ways.

"People who are typically difficult to get on the phone are now engaging with video content, and our webinar numbers have doubled—if not tripled. We have hockey stick growth in a lot of our marketing metrics and it's given us a huge boost."

Matt Trushinksi, Director of Marketing, Miovision

In January 2020, Miovision, a company of roughly 200 employees, announced $120M of new venture capital funding and plans to increase its employee base by 50% to help it keep up with surging demand.

Miovision's story is a great example of how any marketing team can use video throughout the buyer's journey to transform the way it goes to market without having to transform its people or budgets.

PART IV

USING VIDEO
MARKETING IN THE
AWARENESS STAGE

Chapter 15

EARNING ATTENTION AND REACHING NEW AUDIENCES

You can't win a new customer if they don't know you exist.

Brand awareness, the first stage of the buyer's journey, is all about expanding your reach, raising awareness of the problems you solve, and stimulating interest in what you offer.

While getting your brand in front of prospects is a key goal of this stage, it's important to remember that it's not about *you* at this stage. It's all about *them*, the customer.

They're not yet looking for you, they're looking for helpful and thorough answers to their questions, a real solution to a problem they have, or a community of like-minded people who can help.

HOW THE 4 ES OF VIDEO HELP YOU GENERATE MORE AWARENESS

First and foremost, video is the best way to *educate* audiences who are searching for answers at the early stages of discovery.

Not only is video a more effective way to explain complex topics, but it's more consumable and memorable than static content. Given the opportunity, it's more beneficial for both your audience and your brand to have them watch videos at this stage than to read text-based articles.

Second, video is a great way to *engage* new audiences, to pull them into your story, and to maximize their content consumption time.

With video, you can leverage visuals, audio, music, and creative story-telling to give your audience something that is highly relatable and piques their interest. This concept doesn't just apply to video advertisements and promotions, you can make *any* topic more engaging with a thoughtful approach to visual storytelling.

Third, it's the best way to stimulate an *emotional* response from someone who is experiencing your brand for the first time.

Whether it's a fun and creative social video, an inspiring interview, or a highly relatable customer story, invoking an emotional response will increase the chances that new visitors and content consumers will come back for more.

And finally, video is the perfect way to showcase *empathy* and to create a human connection that goes deeper than just your messaging.

This is particularly important at this stage when potential buyers are looking for trustworthy answers to the questions they have. A short video with one of your employees explaining a complex topic beats out any text-based article for showing you truly understand your market.

If I had needed to buy jumper cables on that cold winter morning, you can bet I would have bought them from the individual in that helpful video!

Now, let's dive into practical ideas for how you can use the four Es of video to generate awareness and convert prospects to the next stage.

Chapter 16

HOW TO DRIVE INBOUND TRAFFIC WITH A VISUAL APPROACH TO CONTENT MARKETING

Inbound marketing and content marketing have become a staple of modern marketing programs. The premise of inbound marketing is to publish helpful online content as a means of attracting new visitors to your website, as opposed to using paid advertisements and other forms of "outbound" media to vie for their attention.

The content you publish is typically aligned with the most common questions your audience may be searching for, or the topics they need to learn about while researching possible solutions.

For example, if you run a marketing agency that offers website development services for small businesses, rather than paying for ads that target business owners (most of whom will not be in the market for a new website), you might publish online articles that answer questions like '*What are the best examples of small business websites?*', '*Top website development trends*', or even '*Who are the top marketing agencies for website development?*'.

Small business owners who are actually in the market for website development services will be more likely to discover you by landing on your content via a google search result when kicking off their research.

Inbound marketing has gone through numerous evolutions since it was first introduced nearly 20 years ago with the rise of the company blog, a new home for publishing articles designed to educate the market and attract new leads.

For the first decade, most companies outsourced their blog, leveraging marketing agencies and freelance writers to produce written articles that targeted their key search terms. By 2010, many companies began bringing this function in-house with on-staff writers, or *content marketers*, whose job was to write blog posts to drive as much inbound traffic as possible.

Fast forward a number of years, and changes to Google's search algorithms drove content marketing teams to focus on quality over quantity.

But other important changes have happened over the past few years as well.

Google has been placing greater emphasis on **video content** in its rankings for search results. The expectations of online audiences have also changed, with consumers and business professionals choosing to engage with infographics, podcasts, interactive content, and of course, video, over more traditional forms of written content.

These trends have spurred another important shift for inbound and content marketing anchored around the diversification of content mediums being used to reach audiences.

In today's world of inbound, you need to be delivering content in various formats—including video—if you want to meet the expectations of your audience and keep those leads rolling in.

HOW TO INTEGRATE EDUCATIONAL VIDEOS INTO YOUR INBOUND CONTENT STRATEGY

The most effective types of videos to support inbound marketing programs are educational videos that clearly and *visually* answer the questions your target audiences are asking. It's about leveraging the educational nature of video, while also using it to build a more authentic relationship early in the discovery process.

From a content perspective, the topics you'll want to tackle may be similar to what you're covering in your written content strategy, assuming you have one. After all, the questions being asked aren't any different, you're just changing the way you're going to answer them!

A great place to start is by documenting a list of key topics and SEO search terms that you're already targeting in your inbound strategy, along with any existing guides, e-books, or blog posts that have proven themselves as high performers.

You can also supplement this list by searching YouTube for the types of phrases that your audience may be searching for and seeing which topics are driving high engagement in video format. Start prioritizing your list based on what is currently most relevant for your market, and where you see the greatest opportunity to attract new visitors.

The next step is to think about how you want to approach the style of these videos and how you will leverage on-screen talent, visuals, and audio in the most effective way.

This aspect is what differs the most from a traditional approach to content marketing and writing.

With blog posts, you need to figure out your tone and general writing style, but the overall format and approach are fairly standard and not very flexible. With guides and e-books, you need to add in visual design elements, but these typically stem from your core brand guidelines. With video, you have significantly more freedom in how you approach the visual style, tone, pacing, and overall approach to narratives.

While it may seem a bit daunting at first since there is no simple template to follow, it can also be exciting to generate new ideas and blaze new trails! Remember, video is an amazing opportunity to deliver your messages in ways that are fresh, interesting, and uniquely *you*.

The only real mistake you can make is not trying to create any video at all.

Chapter 17

HOW TO USE VIDEO TO PACKAGE AND PRODUCTIZE YOUR IDEAS IN NEW WAYS

River Pools and Spas is a great example of how a little creativity in your approach to video can go a long way. If you peruse their YouTube channel or website, you'll find a library of hundreds of helpful videos that are truly engaging and authentic.

Many of the topics covered have also been discussed in previous blog posts—how much in-ground pools cost, pros and cons of automatic pool covers, and so on—but video has given them a new opportunity to bring those stories, and their own personalities, to life.

Hang on to that thought, we'll dive deeper into River Pools in just a moment.

When approaching your own video-based thought leadership you'll want to consider how to achieve something similar by being thoughtful about how you approach, package, and productize your ideas using the four Es of video.

It can be as simple as having individuals from your company on camera in "talking head" style videos explaining key topics (educational and empathetic), or as involved as creating a branded episodic video series with a creative set and a variety of guests (engaging and emotional).

You'll also want to consider how to approach your "every day" educational videos—your steady stream of updates that will likely be quicker and more efficient to produce (just like your recurring blog posts)—versus your "hero" videos that will tackle the most important topics and warrant a greater investment in planning and production (like your e-books and guides!).

No matter where you are at in your video journey, there's always a place to start or go next.

Here are five ways you can approach the style of your educational videos designed to generate brand awareness:

- **Talking head** videos have one or two people on camera in a fairly tight shot speaking directly to the camera. They may be delivering a message or explaining a topic, or they may be answering interview-style questions from someone off-camera.

  These can be recorded in almost any location and typically have minimal dependencies on visuals and props. They work well when you have a strong subject matter expert who can clearly deliver your message and keep viewers engaged.

- **Question-and-answer** and **how-to** videos directly address specific questions being asked by your audience. They're typically set up in a way that the title and splash screen make it very clear that this video is all about answering that one question or explaining how to do that one thing.

For example, the title of a video may be "How do I add captions to a LinkedIn video?" and the content immediately dives into answering that question with little or no additional set up. These videos should be short in length, direct and to the point, and take advantage of visuals to make your answer as clear and helpful as possible.

- **Topical deep-dive** videos explore very specific topics that are of interest to sub-segments of your audience. While *talking head* and *how-to* style videos tend to be short, high-level, and targeted at broad audiences, deep-dive videos tend to be longer, more involved, and targeted at a more narrow audience that is looking for detailed information on a specific topic.

  These types of videos may include experts speaking on camera, interviews with thought leaders or customers, or voiceover narratives with different visuals added in during post-production. These videos may also warrant more supporting visuals to help explain the topic, such as the use of a whiteboard or chalkboard, screen capture, or cut-aways to shots of products or services in action.

- **Interview-based** videos bring in one or more people knowledgeable on a subject to present their ideas in an interview-style format. Depending on the nature of your brand, these can be a bit more formal in nature or very casual and impromptu.

  Most businesses are going increasingly casual for these types of videos to provide a sense of authenticity, approachability, and to make the content more trustworthy. The best interview-based videos feel unscripted yet prepared and confident.

- **Episodic series-based** videos are rising in popularity in the business world, offering creative new ways to build your brand, convert followers into subscribers, and boost engagement with audiences on social media and YouTube. In some ways, it's the true realization of brands thinking and acting like media companies.

  Branded episodic video series can follow a number of different formats ranging from a simple weekly series like "Whiteboard Wednesdays" or "Tuesday Tips" to a more involved show-based format like Vidyard's "Creating Connections", IMPACT's "Video School for Marketers", or one of my personal favorites, Andrew Davis' "Loyalty Loop" (go ahead and Google it!). Longer form series-based content is often referred to as 'video podcasts' and in some cases, the audio can be repurposed for a podcast show.

Each of these styles has its own merits, but when it comes to creating video, don't be afraid to think outside the box and to find inspiration from what you enjoy consuming in your personal life.

Try to make video your own, and develop a style and approach that works best for you. But be mindful that "winging it" rarely ever works, no matter how talented your team is on camera.

Planning is the most important phase of any video production. So, going into a shoot with a good sense of the style, approach, and length you're aiming for will go a long way toward guaranteeing your content will hit the mark.

Chapter 18

RIVER POOLS DIVES DEEP WITH VIDEO-BASED THOUGHT LEADERSHIP

Imagine, for a moment, that you're considering putting a new pool into your backyard.

Ahhhh, the cool, refreshing feel of the water on your skin, the unabashed joy of diving in, the soothing and restorative heat of the hot tub, and the countless backyard parties with envious friends, neighbors, and family.

But wait!

You have so many questions you need to answer before you take the plunge. Should you do a fiberglass, vinyl, or concrete pool? Is one type better than the other? What size would be best, and how deep should you go? What about pumps, heaters, solar blankets, vacuums, and…?

The list of questions you'll have will go on and on.

So, like any modern buyer, instead of going to the local pool store where you know they're just going to try to *sell* you, you head straight to Google to start your research. You type in "vinyl vs. fiberglass pools," click the search button, and *boom*, thousands of results at your fingertips.

ANSWERING QUESTIONS VISUALLY

You immediately see that the first search result is an article by River Pools and Spas called "Vinyl Liner Pools vs. Fiberglass Pools: An Honest Comparison." Perfect!

Well, almost. Because, with something like a swimming pool, it really would be nice to *see* what they're talking about, rather than just read it. So, you click on the "video" search results, and sure enough, the first result is a *video* from the same company, River Pools and Spas, with the same title!

In truth, at the time of writing this book, the first *two* videos on the list are both from River Pools and Spas—one directing to their YouTube channel and the second directing to their website.

"Well, they're clearly an authority on the topic," you say to yourself. And then you click the video link.

Five minutes later, a fine gentleman and pool scholar by the name of Cristian Shirilla (who works at River Pools and Spas) has fully educated you on the differences between vinyl and fiberglass pools.

And, despite the fact that River Pools and Spas only sells fiberglass pools, it was an honest and authentic comparison highlighting the pros and cons of each. This experience earns River Pools and Spas, and Cristian himself, immediate trust and credibility.

Not to mention the viewing experience was quite fun and engaging! So, you click to browse their full library of videos and, much to your surprise, you land on the swimming pool Q-and-A equivalent of Netflix.

The River Pools and Spas video library includes hundreds of on-demand videos discussing everything from pool installation costs to how to maintain and replace your pool filter.

Every video is designed to answer a question that a prospective buyer may be asking during the awareness or consideration stage of the buying journey. Every video includes real people from River Pools and Spas discussing an important topic, but they are produced and productized in a number of different and unique ways:

- Some videos are approached in the **question-and-answer** style where the title of the video is the exact question that this video will answer. These videos are optimized for search and SEO, attracting new audiences who are searching for answers to specific questions.

- Some videos take the **show-and-tell** or **topical deep-dive** approach, offering detailed information on a certain problem, concept, or product of interest. For example, their video entitled "River Pools Introduces the Massive T40 Model Pool" provides a comprehensive show-and-tell of what this fiberglass pool looks like and how it works, with Cristian *literally* in the deep end for much of the video.

- And finally, you'll find their flagship **episodic video series** entitled "2 Minutes in the Pool" which offers unique insights in an engaging recurring format. In less than two years, they've published more than 60 episodes, with many receiving *tens of thousands* of views. This series is designed to be highly shareable and to generate more subscribers to their YouTube channel and marketing database.

THE RESULTS OF VIDEO FOR RIVER POOLS AND SPAS SPEAK FOR THEMSELVES

Within two years of making video content a core part of its inbound marketing strategy, River Pools and Spas had nearly tripled the number of inbound leads they were generating and expanded their dealer network by more than 500%.

Not only that, but they are currently the fastest-growing fiberglass swimming pool manufacturer in the world.

Packaging and productizing their ideas in a fresh new way with video not only helped them expand their reach, but also established the team at River Pools and Spas as a trusted advisor in a highly competitive market.

Oh, and one other fact:

Today, their average customer has watched over 20 minutes of their videos before they buy!

Now imagine for a moment, that you're not actually looking to buy a pool, but rather are someone who is in the market for the solution that *your* business sells.

Put yourself in their shoes. If you were to search for a common question they were likely to have during the buying process, would *your business'* content show up in the "all" or "video" search results on Google?

And, if you did start watching your business' video content, would you have the opportunity to go deeper, or would you be inclined to binge on more content or subscribe for updates?

For a healthy dose of inspiration on how to actually do it, check out the River Pools YouTube channel and see how easily "2 Minutes in the Pool" can turn into two hours of content binging.

Chapter 19

VIDEO FOR INBOUND MARKETING CHECKLIST

Whether you're answering a question, teaching others how to accomplish a task, or educating the market on bold new ideas, there's always a way to bring your thought leadership and brand stories to life through the power of video.

"But Tyler, what needs to be on our best practices checklist, so we can maximize the impact of our inbound and content marketing programs with engaging video content?"

I'm so glad you asked!

INBOUND MARKETING CHECKLIST

☐ **Create educational content to answer common questions and address key topics.** Focus on creating helpful videos that answer the key questions your audience may be asking and dive deep into topics that you can provide a unique perspective on. Steer clear of promoting your own products or services, keep your inbound video content focused on your audience, not your own brand.

☐ **Focus more on content value rather than production value.** Make your thought leadership videos feel as helpful and trustworthy as possible. Focus your efforts on providing the greatest value to your viewers via unique insights, expert perspectives, and supporting visuals. Of course, you should still make your video content visually appealing, but don't worry about making it look like a Hollywood production.

☐ **Be intentional with the format, style, and tone of your thought leadership videos.** There are various approaches you can take to the visual style, format, and tone of your thought leadership videos. Plan ahead and be explicit about recording your video in the style of a talking head, question-and-answer, how-to, topical deep-dive, interview-based, or episodic video series. This will help ensure that what you capture on camera aligns with what you want to see in the finished product.

☐ **Plan ahead but keep it natural and conversational.** Capture your thought leadership videos in a way that is natural, conversational, and unscripted. However, that doesn't mean you don't need to plan! Go into every video with a plan for the content you will cover, the visual style and tone you're going for, the target length, and any supporting visual assets you'll use. Your goal is to create something that feels authentic and trustworthy, but also well prepared, clear, and concise.

☐ **Use 4 Es of video to bring your ideas to life.** While your thought leadership videos should always be educational, don't forget about making them engaging, emotional, or empathetic. Video is a richer way to address key topics, not simply a medium to "read your blog post on camera." So, think creatively about how a video could add new dimensions to your content by infusing visuals, stories, energetic body language, humor, personality, relatability, and more.

Chapter 20

HOW TO USE YOUTUBE TO BUILD AN AUDIENCE AND GENERATE LEADS

YouTube isn't merely a destination site for movie trailers and viral videos. In reality, YouTube is a *massive* search engine (second only to Google), where people search for answers and visually learn about different topics.

It's an important channel for businesses to generate awareness and to drive more traffic back to their own website.

While professional YouTubers and media companies use it as a means to generate direct revenue via ad-supported content, businesses now use it to deliver helpful content to their target audiences in a way that supports their inbound marketing and social media programs.

While there's great promise in how any brand can use YouTube to reach new audiences, the reality is that most business' YouTube channels end up becoming their "video retirement home."

It's the place where all of their online video content—thought leadership, product demos, customer testimonials, on-demand webinars, and so on—ends up living out its days. This isn't necessarily a *bad* thing; there's likely no harm in it, but it doesn't capitalize on the opportunity this free marketing channel can offer.

A better way to treat YouTube is as an online channel to build an audience, educate your target market, and generate new leads with a search engine optimization (SEO) mindset. Therefore, there are a few different types of videos that tend to perform the best for most businesses.

To frame those up, let's go back to the four Es of video, and how they can be applied to your YouTube channel:

1. Video is educational: Videos that answer common questions or clearly explain important topics.

2. Video is engaging: Episodic video series that keep audiences coming back for more.

3. Video is emotional: Creative videos that are fun and entertaining, yet still relate to your business and are relevant for your target audience.

"Wait, where's the fourth E?"

Don't worry, I didn't forget it! That final E—*video shows empathy*—should manifest itself in each of the three types listed above by making your YouTube videos so relatable and authentic that people feel like they know you after watching.

Chapter 21

HOW TO USE EDUCATIONAL CONTENT ON YOUTUBE TO ATTRACT MORE VIEWERS

Educational videos are where most businesses start when taking a fresh approach to their YouTube channel.

The good news is that the content you create for your inbound and content marketing programs can often be repurposed here. But to get a good sense of what will work best on YouTube, step back and think critically about what types of questions or keywords people may be searching for on YouTube or Google that you could answer with video content.

Use your SEO analysis tool of choice to see which relevant topics people are searching for specifically on YouTube and which search terms you could effectively service.

Some of the educational videos we discussed in the previous section on inbound marketing should be a perfect fit for your YouTube channel, and there may be new topics you can tackle that seem to be more frequently searched for on YouTube.

Much like with your inbound marketing video strategy, start with a list of the top questions your target audience may be asking and the topics that seem to come up frequently during early stages of the buying journey.

In terms of how you approach the style of these videos, the recommendations from the previous section also apply to your educational videos on YouTube. These can be anything from a talking head style to show-and-tell or interview-based.

But, more often than not, having *real people* in your videos communicating in a natural and authentic way will win out over highly produced "marketing" content when it comes to an audience on YouTube.

HOW TO GROW YOUR AUDIENCE WITH AN ENGAGING EPISODIC VIDEO SERIES

Educational videos are a great way to attract new audiences who are searching for information on YouTube. Once they arrive on your channel, your primary goal is to educate and earn trust.

That said, as a savvy marketer, you'll also want to bring them into an experience that encourages more and more content consumption, creates strong brand affinity, and drives them to subscribe for future updates.

In short, you want them to build a habit around your brand by way of your content.

A great way to drive those desired outcomes is by offering a recurring episodic video series that can leverage YouTube's built-in subscription engine to keep audiences engaged and coming back for more.

This idea gets me fired up because it's the perfect opportunity to get creative, to let down your "corporate" guard, and to create content that you'd be proud to show someone at a party or your next high school reunion.

Going back to River Pools and Spas for a moment, their YouTube channel features a video series called "2 Minutes in the Pool" that gives any visitor an opportunity to binge on a series of content that will educate them on a wide range of topics related to buying or maintaining a swimming pool. And, if pools are something you are truly interested in, you'd be foolish not to subscribe.

In addition to offering a great reason to come back to your channel, there are numerous other benefits of creating your own branded video series.

While individual episodes can be promoted through different channels such as YouTube, social media, email marketing, and even your own website, you can also promote the overall series as a bigger and bolder idea—giving you more opportunities to attract audiences through different types of promotion.

An episodic series also gives prospects a new reason to subscribe to ongoing communications, whether they're subscribing to your YouTube channel, blog, or email newsletter.

Ye olde "fear of missing out" (FOMO) on a great episode is a powerful thing if they've found value in one or more episodes.

Finally, an episodic series gives you the opportunity to build a brand-level relationship with potential buyers that isn't necessarily tied to your corporate brand, but is instead centered around an *idea* or a *movement.* While it may seem scary at first (and counterintuitive to building brand awareness), removing your company's brand from the spotlight can often make your content more trustworthy and shareable, especially on You-Tube and social media.

Here at Vidyard, we've created a number of branded video series, each with its own unique target audience, conversion goal, and promotional strategy.

For the awareness stage, we currently produce three different video shows and we use the audio exports for accompanying podcasts to maximize the reach of each episode.

Video in Focus is a recurring interview-based series targeted at practitioners within businesses who are interested in learning how to use video more effectively to grow their business. This aligns well with our ideal customer profile, giving us new ways to engage this target audience. And yes, many individuals and businesses featured in this book have been guests on the show!

Creating Connections uses a similar format but is targeted at marketing decision-makers and practitioners who care about the latest strategies for connecting with buyers on a more human level. It gives us a platform to discuss a more diverse range of topics and to reach tangential audiences who are not yet looking for a video solution but may at some point in the future.

Last, but certainly not least, **Video Island** is hosted by our internal video producers and provides expert advice for anyone interested in the latest techniques for video production and video editing. Again, this helps us tap into a tangential audience of video creators.

What do all of these different video series have in common? **None of them are about Vidyard or our products.**

Instead, they offer helpful and trustworthy content to our community with YouTube as the primary channel for distribution. And as we move one stage down in the buyer's journey, we offer our **Chalk Talks, Video**

Marketing How-To, and **Video Vednesday** (no, that's not a typo!) series as episodic content that goes deeper on specific areas of interest.

You can find these series for reference and inspiration on the Vidyard YouTube channel.

Chapter 22

CRANES AND AI HAVE NEVER BEEN SO INTERESTING

Unless you're in the construction, steel, or shipbuilding market, you likely don't care that much about cranes, rigging equipment, or fall protection gear. And you've likely never visited **The Lifting and Rigging Channel for Material Handling Professionals** on YouTube.

But if you *are* in one of those industries, this channel is an indispensable source of training and education that just might help you get a better job, improve the efficiency and safety of your business, or even save a life.

As of writing this, it features nearly 200 videos (and counting) across a wide range of topics from across the world of material lifting and rigging. In addition to question-and-answer and deep-dive style videos on specific topics of interest, it includes several branded episodic video series including **Cranes 101, LiftingU,** and (my personal favorite) **The Rigging Professor.**

And since they post a new video every Tuesday and Thursday, it only makes sense to subscribe for updates!

Despite what you might expect, this free-to-access YouTube channel is not run by a member-led association, an educational institution, or an ad-supported media outlet. It's run by Mazzella Companies, a manufacturer and distributor of products for the lifting and rigging market, and a client of Marcus' company, IMPACT.

MAZZELLA TOOK THEIR CONTENT TO THE NEXT LEVEL WITH VIDEO

Having seen success with their online blog and written content strategy, Mazzella Companies decided to ramp up their investment in video-based thought leadership in early 2018 to enhance the value of their content and to exploit a key new marketing channel: YouTube.

In just two years, they amassed more than 75,000 views and a subscriber base of nearly 1,000 individuals. And because they're smart marketers, every video includes the Mazzella Companies brand at some point during the intro or outro, many calls-to-action (including the option to learn more about their products), and a number of their customer case studies are sprinkled into the mix.

Come to learn about overhead cranes, stay to watch **The Rigging Professor,** and then head off to the Mazzella Companies website to learn more about related products and services. It truly is a beautiful thing.

Now, you may be thinking:

"But Tyler, I don't sell physical products like cranes and harnesses, so I'm not sure that I have that much to show and share on a video channel!"

I don't care what type of business or market you are in, I can guarantee you that you *do* have unique and valuable knowledge to share and that there *is* an engaging way to bring it to life via video.

LET LUCIDWORKS SHOW YOU THE WAY

A great example comes from the team at Lucidworks, a B2B software company that sells artificial intelligence (AI) and machine learning (ML) technology.

Talk about something difficult to visualize! I mean, they don't even sell a product or application that you can see or use for yourself, they provide behind-the-scenes technology that powers other applications and services.

So, how did they bring their thought leadership to life through video? By creating an episodic YouTube series called **Lucid Thoughts: For Everyone Curious About AI** that explains what artificial intelligence and machine learning are all about in a way that is clear, engaging, and highly memorable. In fact, it feels like the type of content you might find on Netflix or Disney Plus, and is designed to be equally approachable.

In this case, Lucidworks partnered with video production agency Storyboard Media to develop the concept and produce the episodes, knowing this was a series that they wanted to invest in for future growth. And, thanks to a big response to season one, the show returned with the highly anticipated season two in late 2019 where Tia, queen of the machine learning dragons, discovered that her uncle…

Oh, wait. Sorry, no spoilers!

You'll have to check out the Lucid Thoughts YouTube channel to see how the story unfolds—and for some seriously great inspiration.

Chapter 23

HOW TO STRIKE AN EMOTIONAL CHORD WITH BRAND ENTERTAINMENT

The idea of brand entertainment is becoming more common in the business world as marketers look for new ways to stand out from the unending digital noise. And while brand entertainment can be a difficult thing to get right, the payoff can be significant if you hit the right note and deliver something that is truly shareworthy.

Unfortunately, there is no prescriptive formula for how to use humor and entertainment in today's business world. That means you'll need to rely on your creativity and willingness to experiment—especially if you don't have the budget to hire a creative agency.

But it's important to understand that brand entertainment isn't reserved just for big consumer brands, which is where our minds typically go when thinking about entertainment. It's something that any business—big or small, B2C or B2B—can weave into its personality, and YouTube can be a great channel for experimentation.

One of my favorite examples of using humor in B2B is a video from helpdesk software vendor Zendesk video called, "I Like It When He Gives Me the Business."

This video uses an elderly couple to represent the relationship between a company and its clients, reflecting on their courtship and how things have evolved over time. The dialogue is incredibly entertaining, and it's when the elderly wife says "I love it when he gives me the business" that you find yourself truly laughing out loud. By the end of the video, you can't help but click the LIKE button and then head to Zendesk.com to learn more about what they do.

 To appreciate the video, you really need to watch it—along with other great examples—and you can find it at **www.thevisualsale.com**.

The Zendesk example may not be fair for your businesses as it was scripted and produced by a creative agency on what was likely a sizable budget. But another great example from the team here at Vidyard is a two-part video series we created with a $130 budget called **SalesFails**.

We were looking for a way to build awareness of our new personal video messaging tool for sales reps. Through some iterative team brainstorming, we landed on the idea of poking fun at the "villain" in our story, who was represented by those bad text-based prospecting emails that we all know and hate.

I'm sure you know them all too well. The faceless sales emails that come out of a copy-and-paste template claiming they can help you generate 30% more revenue, and all you need to do is book a 15-minute call?

We decided to have some fun and make it highly relatable by doing a parody of Jimmy Kimmel's recurring "Mean Tweets" skit, wherein he asks celebrities to read mean tweets about themselves and react on camera.

In our version, **SalesFails,** we had people read bad sales prospecting emails out loud on camera and react in a similar way. The first video was shot with all internal employees and received a great response from our audience. So, we created a second "celebrity edition" with influencers from across our community reading and reacting to some of the worst sales emails they have ever received.

The resulting video was hugely entertaining but it also shone a bright light on the problem we were helping to solve. In fact, many people shared it with others saying things like, "I bet you can relate to this!" or "OMG so true!"

Through the power of social sharing and some helpful promotion by the influencers (which they were happy to do given the fun and humorous nature of the content), the videos reached thousands of people on our YouTube and social media channels, far surpassing the reach of most content assets we've produced as a B2B software company.

 You can watch the videos for yourself on **www.thevisualsale.com** to see if you think they were entertaining enough to be shareworthy.

Chapter 24

LUCIDCHART REACHES MILLIONS WITH B2B BRAND ENTERTAINMENT

Inspiration can come from just about anywhere when it comes to brand entertainment. Another great example comes from Lucidchart, a B2B software company who provides online tools for diagramming, data visualization, and team collaboration.

What started as an idea within an internal Slack channel called **#BadIdeas** is now a hilarious YouTube video series that has garnered more than 20 million views. Yes, 20 *million* views—not to mention more than 300,000 subscribers! Not bad for a B2B software company.

Of course, while it's safe to say that not all of these viewers are within Lucidchart's target market, one of the business outcomes they've seen, which I'll share in a moment, is nothing to laugh at.

But first, how the heck did they do this? Which big creative agency did they work with to develop and produce such a viral series? **None.**

They did it themselves on a minimal budget, and it happened because they already had a culture that embraced creativity, humor, transparency, and video. Their exceptionally funny (and surprisingly educational) You-Tube series called **Lucidchart Explains the Internet** offers dozens of one-minute videos explaining different topics, concepts, or pop culture movements in a way that is fast-paced, very fun, and oddly addictive.

Some of my favorites include:

- "Bunnos, Buns, and Wabbits: Internet Names for Bunnies Explained"
- The epic "Star Wars Relationships Explained"
- . . . and the incredibly helpful "Fortnite Explained in 60 Seconds"

While the topic of each video has nothing to do with Lucidchart's products, the big reveal after 55 seconds is that the tool they used to illustrate and visualize the content in the video was none other than Lucidchart!

So, not only did you just learn how Luke Skywalker is related to Princess Leia, you discovered a great new tool that could help your team at work create equally awesome diagrams, charts, and data visualizations for greater collaboration.

What's more, thanks to all of the sharing and fanfare, Lucidchart's product overview and tutorial videos have been viewed more than 1 million times.

I'm hopeful the next video they publish will be called "Lucidchart Explains How to Do Brand Entertainment Right." Until then, however, I encourage you to check out a few episodes of **Lucidchart Explains the**

Internet to learn about doggos, bitcoin, danger noodles, and video-based brand entertainment.

Chapter 25

YOUTUBE VIDEO CHECKLIST

YouTube offers an amazing channel to share bold ideas and to expand your online audience. But it takes more than a "post-and-pray" approach to generate real value from your YouTube channel. Here are the most important best practices to follow when building out your YouTube channel strategy:

☐ **Define the goals of your YouTube channel to guide your content plan.** Don't let your YouTube channel become your video retirement home! Be explicit in planning out the goals for your YouTube channel and the type of content that will help you achieve those goals. Most companies use YouTube as a channel to generate awareness, expand their following, and create more inbound traffic to their website.

☐ **Create educational content to answer common questions and address key topics.** Start by focusing on helpful video content that answers the key questions your audience may be asking and dives deep into topics that you can provide a unique and valuable perspective on. Also, as tempting as it may be, steer clear of promoting your own products or services, so your content remains trustworthy and shareable.

☐ **Create an episodic video series to drive subscriptions and sharing.** Consider producing one or more episodic video series and creating a dedicated playlist on your YouTube channel for each. Prompt viewers to subscribe to your YouTube channel to be notified when new episodes are released, and encourage them to like and share the series if they find it to be valuable. And don't forget to offer links back to your main website or blog for those who want to learn even more.

☐ **Use brand entertainment to be memorable and shareable.** Video is the perfect medium to let your guard down and have some fun, and YouTube can be a great channel to test out brand entertainment. Consider fun ways to use video to play off pop culture trends, to make people laugh during different holidays throughout the year, or to bring your messaging to life through humorous skits and storytelling.

☐ **Use playlists to organize your content in a way that maximizes engagement.** Playlists are a great way to organize videos on your YouTube channel and to help viewers discover the most relevant and related content. Establish categories or themes for your YouTube videos up-front (i.e. how-to videos, FAQs, [Topic] 101, customer stories, and so on) and create a playlist for each. Assign new videos to the appropriate playlist to keep your channel organized in a way that will maximize engagement.

Chapter 26

HOW TO EXPAND YOUR SOCIAL MEDIA REACH WITH ENGAGING VIDEO

The rise of video on social media has been nothing short of extraordinary. Facebook and Snapchat have reported 8 billion and 10 billion video views respectively every day on their platforms—and that was back in 2016, the most recent year the two have provided this data.

The following year saw Facebook and Twitter launch live video services and, in 2018, LinkedIn introduced support for video aimed at business professionals.

During this time an important trend was revealed in the market, influencing how social networks now treat video content:

Video was making people stick around longer.

The data has shown that when people interact with social media posts that include video, their overall engagement time increases significantly. In fact, Facebook recently reported that posts with video generate five times higher engagement time compared to posts with static content.

For the social media networks, longer engagement time means more revenue thanks to their ad-supported business models, so they are highly motivated to push more video content to their members—and that's exactly what they're doing.

For businesses that get on board, it can be a double win. Posts with video are likely to drive higher engagement and are also more likely to be pushed to your followers' feeds. More reach and more engagement is the foundation of a strong social media strategy, so without video, you're lacking a critical component.

But it takes more than posting any old video to see success with these channels.

Today, many businesses simply use their social channels to share the content they are already creating for other purposes. For example, they produce a great new explainer video for their website or a new video ad for their digital channels, and they push it out on social as well.

That's how you do social *video, right?! Bring on the views!*

Well, not quite.

The bigger opportunity is to create a proactive social video strategy that identifies the types of videos, both existing and new, that will help you generate the greatest engagement on your social media channels.

The good news is that, on social media, authenticity trumps production value, so most net-new content can be created with just your smartphone or webcam and a little bit of creativity.

PUTTING A SOCIAL SPIN ON YOUR EXISTING THOUGHT LEADERSHIP

Reduce, reuse, re-engage!

If you're already creating thought leadership videos to support other aspects of your marketing program, repurposing these on social media can be a great place to start for your social video strategy.

Much like YouTube, social media is a channel for being helpful, earning trust, and building relationships with audiences who may not yet be invested in your brand. Therefore you should focus your efforts on sharing video content that is truly helpful and shareable, steering clear of content that feels like "marketing" or "selling."

Or, more to the point, pumping out product demos and pricing videos on social media is a great way to lose followers and generate a negative impression of your brand.

When repurposing thought leadership videos—*or the new ones you'll create based on the ideas in previous chapters of this book!*—be mindful that much of your engagement on social will come from people discovering your content, often unexpectedly, while perusing their feeds.

In other words, they're not looking for you, you're looking for them.

This is a different paradigm from your website or YouTube channel where people are actively looking for information and are expecting to spend time-consuming content. On social media, prioritize sharing shorter-form thought leadership videos that can quickly capture attention and be consumed in their entirety in five minutes or less—ideally, no more than two or three minutes.

You can also create shorter versions of existing long-form thought leadership videos to use on your social media channels. Someone may choose to ignore an eight minute video on their social feed as it's too much of a disruption, but may engage with a two-minute version of that same content that offers some quick highlights and takeaways.

This can be done by editing longer-form content down to some key messages and highlights and then linking out to the full-length video for those who want to dive deeper.

Another consideration when repurposing existing videos is to make the introduction really count. The first five seconds is when someone will decide whether or not they'll stop scrolling and commit to paying attention.

If your existing video doesn't include a catchy intro to draw people in, make some small updates to spice up the beginning to stimulate curiosity!

You can record a new scene for the start of your video where you immediately ask a big question that will get answered in the video. *"Are you wondering how the best companies retain top talent while paying them less? Find out in today's video, 'Retain Those Brains!'"* Or you can feature a short, catchy "pull quote" from somewhere in the video right at the beginning as a teaser for what's to come.

In either case, you can add a simple graphic (maybe even with some stock music) to transition from the introduction to the main video, or simply cut right to the main content to keep things moving. Put yourself in the shoes of your audience and consider what would make *you* stop and watch if you saw your video start auto-playing in your social media feed.

Chapter 27

HOW TO CREATE SOCIAL-FIRST THOUGHT LEADERSHIP VIDEOS

Beyond sharing your existing videos on your social media channels, start creating new video-based thought leadership that is purposefully and specifically built for social media audiences.

In other words, think about what types of videos you would create if your only goals were to maximize engagement and sharing on your social media channels. How would that impact the type of content you create, how long would those videos be, and how you would approach the narratives? What type of content would you expect to perform the best on LinkedIn vs. Facebook vs. Twitter vs. Instagram, and how would that impact what you create?

When creating new thought leadership videos for your social channels, you can use some of the same frameworks and styles discussed in the previous chapters, such as talking head, how-to, episodic series, and so on. However, there are some important differences to consider when creating content for social media audiences.

First, these videos should be **short in length,** respecting the fact that many viewers will be discovering your content while scrolling through their feeds. So, keep your social-first videos less than three minutes in length. If you simply have too much to share, split your content up into multiple videos!

Second, be mindful of how you will approach **the first five seconds** of your video. On social media, your video will often autoplay within your audience's feed, giving you a precious few moments to pique their interest before they continue on. Start your videos by posing an important question, challenging conventional wisdom, or using eye-catching visuals to encourage your followers to tune in for the rest.

For great examples of how to do this well, just follow my co-author Marcus Sheridan on LinkedIn to see how he approaches his social-first thought leadership videos.

Chapter 28

HOW TO ACTIVATE YOUR EMPLOYEES AND BRAND ADVOCATES WITH SOCIAL VIDEO

In addition to sharing pre-recorded thought leadership videos, capitalize on the nature of social media with timely videos from your own employees and brand advocates. After all, the real power of social media is in its ability to share timely information with trusted communities of interest, right?

More and more business leaders and brand advocates are turning to video on networks like LinkedIn and Facebook to offer insights on timely market trends, share company news, or provide a weekly dose of inspiration.

These videos are typically recorded in a cheap-and-cheerful way using a smartphone, webcam, or inexpensive DSLR camera with little or no post-production editing.

Sometimes it takes only one take to get it right, and other times it may take a few. But the real power in these videos lies in the fact that they are unscripted and genuine. They build rapport by showcasing your executives and employees as real people and earn trust by demonstrating their expertise and passion.

When empowering your people to build their voice on social media with video, there are a number of things to keep in mind to guarantee their content will help you further relationships with existing audiences, while also attracting new followers.

From a content creation standpoint, it's important that these videos don't appear overly produced or scripted. Once more with feeling, authenticity, and simplicity trump production value with this video style.

From a topical perspective, you may wish to share an update on some timely market news, or you may have a list of predetermined topics that are relevant to your market where you discuss one each week in a short social video.

No matter what your approach is, the most important thing is to have *consistency in your frequency* of social video creation and sharing.

Your first video may only capture a few dozen views, but as more people spend more time with your content week over week, the networks will reward you by amplifying future posts. Ideally, try to have your key brand advocate(s) record and share at least one video per week.

While this may seem daunting for many executives, you can make this easy by preparing a list of topics ahead of time and encouraging them to record one video each week using their smartphone or webcam — or even pre-recording a number of them in batches. You could even call it something like "Tuesday Tips" to make it more interesting and to act as a forcing function to generate content weekly.

It may feel difficult and unnatural at first, but it won't be long before it feels even easier than writing an email.

From a sharing and distribution perspective, these videos can be shared on your company's social profile or page, but ideally, they are also shared on your employee's or brand advocate's own personal social media profiles. In doing so, you can expand the reach of your content while also enabling your brand advocate to become a trusted voice in the community.

On social media, people tend to follow—and *trust*—real people over brands.

Honest-to-goodness human beings are more trustworthy, more interesting and, well, more real!

Chapter 29

SOCIAL VIDEO CHECKLIST

No matter what types of videos you share on social media, the key to success is to recognize the unique ways in which audiences consume content on social channels and to optimize your approach accordingly.

Refer to the checklist below for best practices on how to ensure you get the most out of every social video post:

☐ **Grab their attention in the first five seconds.** Your video will often autoplay within your audience's feed as they are scrolling through. So, ask yourself how you might use visuals and your script to get their attention within those precious first few seconds. Start by asking a big question (i.e. "How do the *best* companies out there retain top talent?"), challenging conventional wisdom (i.e. "The best companies don't retain top talent with higher salaries"), or using creative visuals to pique their interest.

If you are sharing a longer-form thought leadership video that was originally created for your website or YouTube channel, do some small edits to add a new scene or a compelling "'pull quote" at the very beginning to catch people's attention and to create a sense of curiosity.

☐ **Use a visual style that is interesting to watch and includes some type of movement.** Humans are visually drawn toward two things: a sense of movement and the human face. This is why walk-and-talk videos can be hard to ignore.

Using visuals and a sense of movement is particularly important on social media where you are competing with so many other pieces of content and need to "attention hack." When creating a video that includes an individual talking to the camera, use expressive body language or even hard cuts to different camera angles to gain attention and draw viewers in.

☐ **Don't forget that shorter is better (generally speaking) for videos on social media.** Prioritize creating and/or sharing thought leadership videos that are less than three minutes in length to maximize the chances that your audience will engage and share. On social media, people are typically expecting to consume shorter bursts of information, and they may not engage at all if they see the video is more than five minutes in length.

If you have too much to share, that's OK! Break your message up into multiple videos or create a multi-part video series! Then save your longer-form videos for YouTube and your website.

☐ **Remember, not all social networks are created equal.** Be mindful that each social network has its own restrictions on video lengths and formats. Also be considerate of the unique use-case and content consumption style on each social network, and how that may impact the type of video that will best resonate with your audience.

For example, a video formatted in 16:9 landscape may work best on LinkedIn and Facebook, while vertical or square dimensions may feel more natural on Instagram. Similarly, a three-minute educational video may work well on LinkedIn while a much shorter creative "story" may work on Instagram. While that's a lot to keep track of, the good news is that there are various apps and services available for exporting your videos in different sizes and dimensions for different social media channels.

☐ **Transcribe and caption your videos.** Most people will begin watching your social videos with their volume turned off, so it's important to ensure they can follow along via closed captions. This is typically done by transcribing the audio into a text-based SRT file, which can then be edited and uploaded along with your video.

Again, there are various apps and services available for generating transcriptions and SRT files, as well as others that will transcribe your audio and bake your transcription right into the video file itself with overlaid graphics. This eliminates the need to upload a separate SRT file, while also giving you the option to make your font larger and more prominent.

☐ **Upload your video natively rather than linking out to another page.** If possible, upload the video file to the native player within each social network rather than linking out to a YouTube player or a landing page with that video. Only with native video can you leverage the autoplay capabilities within each network and maximize the chances of your post showing up in the feeds of your followers.

This can be done by uploading the video directly via the interface of each social media network, or it can be pushed into a native player via online video hosting platforms that support this functionality.

Chapter 30:

HOW TO TAKE YOUR EVENTS ONLINE WITH WEBINARS AND VIRTUAL EVENTS

If you're part of a B2B marketing or sales team, chances are you're familiar with online presentations in the form of webinars and virtual events.

Love 'em or hate 'em, these live video formats prove time and again that people are willing to give you their two most precious resources — their *time* and *contact information* — in exchange for valuable, relevant online content.

Webinars and virtual events have been common in many industries for years, but their popularity recently skyrocketed in response to travel restrictions, remote work policies, and event cancellations resulting from the coronavirus (COVID-19) pandemic.

Most live events — including industry trade shows, customer conferences, and targeted meet-ups — have now moved to an online format.

Educational webinars are replacing in-person events as a means of generating new leads or engaging current prospects. And many businesses are now learning how to run their own online events as a way to stay connected with customers and prospects in the years ahead.

Those businesses are also discovering that online events can produce far greater value than live conferences at a fraction of the cost, leaving them wondering why it took so long to make this change in the first place.

Whether you're new to running online events or a seasoned webinar pro, now is the time to take a fresh look at how these tactics can help redefine your marketing strategy in an increasingly virtual world.

HOW TO DELIVER ENGAGING AND IMPACTFUL ONLINE WEBINARS

In a nutshell, an online webinar (derived from the latin phrase *webicus seminarium*) is a presentation or moderated discussion delivered in an online virtual format.

Unlike the other video types discussed thus far, webinars are typically 30 to 60 minutes in length, delivered via a live broadcast at a specific time, and may involve an interactive question-and-answer session with audience members. They can feature one or more presenters, may include slides, videos, or screenshares, and can be run by a third-party provider or your own business as a means of generating new leads or engaging your current audience.

Reflecting on the four Es of video, you should focus your webinars on **educating** viewers by sharing unique insights and perspectives, and being

empathetic to your audience by featuring speakers and examples they can closely relate to.

That being said, while education and empathy will be critical to your success, the best webinars I've attended are those that also feel energetic and fast-paced, fun and collaborative, and oozing with passion. Like that one time Marcus Sheridan jumped through my monitor and into my home, shook me by the shoulders, and woke me up to the idea of 'they ask, you answer'! If you've seen Marcus present on a webinar, you know what I'm talking about. His energy and passion are infectious, drawing you in and inspiring you to take action from thousands of miles away.

Or, put another way, that best webinars are those that are also **engaging** and **emotional**.

The keys to nailing all four Es in your webinars are to choose the right topics, the right delivery format, and perhaps most of all, the right speakers.

The webinars I've enjoyed the most are those that feature a relevant industry analyst, researcher, or practitioner at an organization similar to my own. They share proven ideas and personal tips while speaking directly to the viewers — animated body language and all — to create an engaging and inspiring experience.

There are countless resources available online to learn how to host your own webinars, so I won't repeat the fundamentals here.

However, as you approach your own webinar strategy, consider the recommendations below. In following them, you will guarantee the greatest possible value to both your attendees and your business.

1. Have a clear goal and target attendee in mind

In addition to choosing an appropriate topic, clearly identify the goal of your webinar and the top three takeaways or next steps you want attendees to walk away with. One of my favorite ways to document this is to write the goal and key takeaways down in the desired language of your attendees.

For example, "By the end of this webinar, I will be able to use video in the sales process. Specifically, I will know what tools I need, how to use video in each stage of the sales process, and measure the success of my sales videos."

Also, identify your ideal target attendee and build your plan with *that attendee or persona* in mind. What are their biggest fears, questions, or concerns around a given topic? Why is it important to them? Where is this ideal buyer in their buyer's journey?

Clearly documenting the target attendee persona and explicit goals of the webinar will help ensure you generate the outcomes that both you, and your attendees, had in mind.

2. Choose amazing speakers

I said it before, and I'll say it again: If you want to put on an incredible webinar your ideal buyers won't soon forget, you must bring in amazing speaking talent. This isn't negotiable.

The best speakers are not only knowledgeable and insightful, they're adept at bringing personality, energy, and passion to their presentations. They understand how to draw in an audience by posing great questions, creating curiosity, and telling interesting stories that build anticipation and hold attention for 30 minutes to an hour.

If you feature the wrong speaker — those who simply read back the text on their slides or drown viewers in a thinly veiled sales pitch — your attendees will tune out or drop-off after the first five minutes.

Also, while you may be tempted to feature speakers from your own company, you shouldn't always. In fact, I encourage you to invite industry experts, analysts, practitioners, and heck, even your own customers to be the star of your show. It may sound strange at first, but in doing so, you'll maximize the relatability, relevance, and trust of your content.

3. Get creative with your format

Most webinars follow a familiar and consistent format. They're 45 minutes to an hour in length, they include a prepared slide deck with one or two presenters, and they allow audience members to submit questions to be answered at the end.

Don't be shy to break the mold and experiment with new approaches! Consider moderated discussions instead of prepared presentations. Test out shorter formats such as 15- or 25-minute webinars. Go beyond slides with screenshares, embedded videos, or presenters using whiteboards and flip charts to explain ideas!

Bottom line, I encourage you to get creative, apply some fresh thinking, and never be afraid to try something new.

4. Use the on-demand recording for ongoing value

The value of your webinar doesn't end when the live broadcast is over. In most industries, only 20% to 25% of webinar registrants actually show up to watch the live session.

So, what about that other 75% of registrants, and the thousands of others who you know could get value? Leverage the on-demand recording as a hot new content asset to re-engage those who couldn't attend live, to attract new viewers who may have missed the previous promotions, and to generate more engagement in the months ahead.

(Also, by a show of hands, how many of you have registered for a webinar only ever intending to watch it on-demand and not live?)

Host your on-demand webinars on your website or a landing page, promote them in outbound marketing campaigns, and add them as calls-to-action within your email nurture programs and in your content.

For more tips on webinar technology providers and how to run an engaging webinar, refer to the following article on the Vidyard blog: **www.vidyard.com/blog/webinars**

HOW TO TAKE YOUR IN-PERSON CONFERENCES AND MEETUPS ONLINE WITH VIRTUAL EVENTS

When the coronavirus pandemic hit in early 2020, travel restrictions and social distancing became a universal reality virtually overnight.

It was an incredible shock to the system for those running in-person events, forcing conference organizers, event planners, and brands around the world to rethink their approach to bringing people together. Some events were simply cancelled. Others were postponed. But many decided to take their events online with a digital-only virtual experience.

While the overall approach to the events had to be adapted to better suit an online format, the results seen by many of those companies have been very interesting to say the least.

Virtual events not only worked, but they allowed event organizers to reach a broader audience at a fraction of the cost and complexity. In some cases, these virtual event experiences also opened up new opportunities for speakers and attendees to interact.

Now don't get me wrong, I'm a huge proponent of in-person events. Bringing people together, meeting up face-to-face, and creating shared experiences tied to your brand is a very powerful thing.

Virtual events can not, and will not, replace live events.

However, during the pandemic, business teams in nearly every market quickly discovered that virtual events can be a highly effective alternative or complement to their live events strategy. They proved that the technology to power digital experiences for live, video-based presentations, online networking, interactive question-and-answer sessions, and impromptu "meetings" at virtual vendor booths was not only fully capable, but was also able to be used at scale and managed by an individual marketer.

And, perhaps most importantly, it exposed the fact that virtually any business — big or small — can host their own virtual event on a wide range of budgets.

Like webinars, there are countless resources available online to learn how to host your own virtual event. Many of the same technologies used to power webinars can be used to create virtual event experiences.

As you consider planning your own virtual event, consider the following recommendations to minimize your resource investments while maximizing the value for all parties involved.

1. Understand your "must-have" and "nice-to-have" features

Virtual events can come in many shapes and sizes. They can be as simple as a series of online webinars, or as complex as a full-blown virtual summit with attendee networking, sponsors, virtual booths, scavenger hunts, and live rock concerts!

Well, maybe not the concerts.

Be mindful that as you add more functionality and complexity to your event, you will likely be adding to the cost for the supporting technology and the required resource investment to implement and manage. To figure out what's best for you, ask yourself the following questions:

How many attendees are we expecting to join the live event?

Is it important for some, or all, of the presentations to be delivered live?

How important is live interactivity and networking between attendees?

What can we do to differentiate our event or to align it with our brand promise?

Will we have event sponsors, and if so, what are their goals and expectations?

What is our budget and what resources do we have to support the event?

2. Have a plan for managing registrations and attendee communications

You'll need a system in place to manage attendee registrations as well as outbound communications before, during, and after the event. The more targeted, personal, and timely the communications the better.

For smaller virtual events, you may be able to manage these using your existing tools. For example, using HubSpot, Marketo, or Salesforce for email-based promotion and attendee registration. However, this can quickly become a complex and resource-intensive task for larger scale virtual events.

One of the greatest benefits of using a purpose-built virtual event platform is that they offer turnkey solutions for attendee registration, preferred session sign-up, calendar invites, timely reminders, and templated pre- and post-event communications. These capabilities can not only save you time and effort, but can help to increase the number of attendees who participate in the live event.

3. Partner up to expand your reach

Like a live in-person event, consider recruiting partners and complementary vendors to support, or sponsor, your virtual event. Sponsors can be a great channel to promote your event to a broader audience, helping you expand your reach and maximize exposure.

A great way to entice sponsors for your event is to offer a select group of partners free sponsorship with the ability to host a session and access the attendee list, in exchange for promoting the event to their audience and driving additional registrations.

You can also even create incentives by offering different levels of lead sharing based on how many attendees they drive to the event.

4. Get creative with your format

Like online webinars, there is no single formula for a successful virtual event. They can be a half-day, full-day, or multi-day affair. Content can be delivered as live sessions, on-demand recordings, or a mix of both. Networking and question-and-answer sessions can happen in many different ways.

Also, don't forget that people still like to have some fun and join in on shared experiences, even when they're remote! Get creative, and don't be shy — speak with a few virtual event technology vendors for tips on how to make your event stand out, and how to maximize engagement with your very real audience.

For more tips on virtual event technology providers and how to run a successful online event, refer to the following article on the Vidyard blog: **www.vidyard.com/blog/online-events**

Chapter 31:

VIDYARD'S VIRTUAL EVENT EMERGES AS TOP DEMAND GENERATOR

I clearly recall one of my earliest conversations with Vidyard's co-founder and CEO, Michael Litt, back in January of 2014. It was a cold and sunny winter's day in downtown Kitchener, Ontario, and we were meeting up for coffee to discuss my first week as the head of marketing at Vidyard.

We chatted about the logistics, the people, and the budgets. As our conversation turned to marketing and sales strategy, I clearly recall how Michael focused on two related themes as priorities for the business:

The fastest way to scale our business is to be the leader of the video marketing movement, to build and support a global community of marketers and creators, and to help that community be successful by learning from us and each other.

Build a community.

Lead the movement.

And thus the core of our marketing strategy was born, and it remains the same to this very day.

Since then, we've grown from 30 employees to more than 200, and the size of our customer base and community has grown more than one hundred-fold. But the core ethos remains unchanged.

To build that community and create that movement, we've embraced many of the strategies covered thus far in this book, using both video and other forms of content to establish ourselves as the leader in our space.

We've invested in hundreds of blog posts, guides, videos, infographics, research reports, assessments, and podcast episodes to share our knowledge across a myriad of digital channels. We've also run hundreds of webinars, sponsored key industry events, and hosted our own user conferences and meetups.

But, in 2018, we invested in a new initiative that quickly became the single most impactful program as it relates to audience reach, new lead generation, *and* new pipeline development. It was our virtual event called **Fast Forward** — and what an appropriate name that was!

Fast Forward was originally conceived as an alternative to running our annual in-person live event. While our live events were highly impactful and truly memorable, they were also extremely costly to host and resource intensive to manage. In 2018 we decided to take a break and to host a virtual event as an alternative.

Basing the approach on our experience with live events, we incorporated the following elements into a two-day virtual format:

More than 30 unique presentations across multiple content tracks to appeal to multiple personas and attendee types.

A small number of live presentations, or keynotes, with high-impact speakers and a larger number of on-demand sessions accessible during the event.

A dedicated track for our customers offering deep dive sessions on our products as well as best practices from other users.

Ten sponsors and media partners who each promoted the event to their communities in exchange for lead sharing and an opportunity to host a presentation.

By having a wide range of content to appeal to multiple personas, as well as a strong group of partners and sponsors to help promote the event beyond our existing audience, Fast Forward attracted more than 1,500 registrations and more than 700 actively engaged attendees in its first year.

And the total cost to run the event was less than $10,000.

Following the event, we saw a large volume of newly qualified leads convert into new customers. Throughout the following year, we repurposed all those great on-demand sessions in various ways across our blog, email nurturing sequences, social media, and outbound marketing campaigns to extract even more value.

In its second year, Fast Forward attracted more than 2,500 registrants. In 2020 we're working on expanding this to multiple virtual events throughout the year with a goal of engaging and educating 5,000 members of our community as we continue to build, and lead, the video movement.

As for 2021 and beyond, the possibilities are endless!

Chapter 32:

WEBINAR AND VIRTUAL EVENT CHECKLIST

Webinars and virtual events can be powerful tools for creating awareness, engaging your audience, and generating new leads for your sales team. With the right topics, speakers, and formats, they can offer the next best thing to a live event or presentation.

Here are the most important best practices to follow when building out your webinar and virtual event strategy:

☐ **Have a clear goal and attendee persona in mind**
In addition to choosing a great topic your audience will love, have a clear goal and set of outcomes or next steps defined before planning out the details. Identify your target audience and be sure to select a speaker and content format that is most likely to resonate with that attendee or persona.

☐ **Choose amazing speakers who can keep a digital audience engaged**
Choosing the right speakers for your presentations and moderated discussions will make all the difference in how your content is received. Identify speakers who are not only relevant and relatable to your audience, but can also deliver their message in a clear, engaging, and interesting way.

The only thing harder than keeping a live audience engaged for a 30-minute (or longer)presentation is keeping a remote audience engaged!

☐ **Stay creative and fresh in your approach to the format**
Don't get caught in the trap of thinking your webinars and virtual events need to follow a prescribed formula. Consider different approaches to session lengths, presentation styles, supporting visuals, audience interactivity, peer-to-peer chat, and more.

For virtual events, online experiential elements to complement your presentations can keep your audience engaged and involved.

☐ **Leverage your partner community to expand your reach**
Whether you are hosting a webinar or running a full-fledged virtual event, look to your partners and complementary vendors as a way to increase your return on investment. Partnering up with other organizations can quickly expand the organic reach of your promotions and create a win-win experience for both businesses.

☐ **The value doesn't end when the live session is over**

Create a plan to leverage the on-demand recordings of your webinar and virtual event sessions for ongoing value long after the event is over. Repurpose these presentations to re-engage your community via your blog, online resource center, email marketing, and social media channels. Re-promote the on-demand versions on their own landing pages to generate new leads and qualify prospects all year long.

PART V

USING VIDEO MARKETING IN THE CONSIDERATION AND DECISION STAGES

Chapter 33

EXPLAINING YOUR VALUE AND STAYING TOP-OF-MIND

The awareness stage of the buying journey is the part of marketing that tends to get the most visibility and the most glory.

Content created for awareness is expected to get a broader reach and lots of shares, and you may spend advertising dollars to promote this content to new audiences. You can be fun and creative, and can experiment with different messaging on different channels.

However, this kind of content is only the tip of the iceberg when it comes to modern marketing. In today's digital, self-serve world, marketers have just as big a role to play in converting brand-aware prospects into actively engaged buyers.

As potential buyers move into consideration and decision phases, they are now familiar with your brand and your new goal is to generate real demand for your product or service. Your primary channels for engaging during these stages include your website, your blog and learning center, email marketing, automated nurtures, and your direct sales team.

Throughout these stages, your focus should be on clearly explaining what you do and how you do it, showcasing the pains you solve and the benefits you offer in a way that is relevant and relatable to different buyers, proactively answering frequently asked questions, and building a personal connection between your prospects and the people within your business.

So yes, you effectively need to think and act like a great sales rep, but to do it at scale.

Thank goodness you have video content to help you out, right?

MAKING VIDEO YOUR SALES REP WHO NEVER SLEEPS

Much like during the awareness stage, video's unique characteristics are what make it so effective throughout the consideration and decision stages.

Remember, the latest analyst research suggests the majority of the consideration stage is now done in a self-service manner using online digital resources. Yet this is also the stage at which providing clarity around what you do is so important, and establishing an emotional connection with your brand and your people is imperative.

Businesses can no longer rely exclusively on sales reps to communicate their unique value proposition, answer frequently asked questions, provide demonstrations, or move deals forward by establishing a more personal connection. More and more, these are becoming the job of marketing—and this is where video content can truly shine as your *sales rep that never sleeps*.

As you think about your video content strategy during these phases, focus on video's abilities to educate, to create an emotional connection, and to showcase empathy for your buyer's needs.

Educating with video during these stages is all about explaining, in a clear and memorable way, what you do, how you do it, and what makes you unique. Creating an emotional connection is about building brand affinity, making your prospects feel inspired and excited, and creating a sense of urgency to move forward quickly. Being empathetic is about showcasing that you truly understand their problems in ways they can relate to, introducing them to the real people in your business, and earning their trust.

If you execute these principles effectively, you can not only convert and win more customers, but you can improve the efficiency of your entire marketing and sales process.

Chapter 34

HOW TO MAKE YOUR WEBSITE AN INSIGHTFUL AND DELIGHTFUL CONVERSION MACHINE

Many businesses consider their website to be one of the most critical channels—if not *the most critical channel*—for accelerating demand during the consideration stage of the buyer's journey.

Your website is the one destination that can make or break the decision for someone to continue learning about your solution. In fact, a poor or confusing website experience can kill an opportunity before you even knew it existed, whereas a great experience can turn the most skeptical prospect into a believer.

Yet many businesses still struggle to make their website a modern destination that is both insightful and delightful for online visitors. What's more, very few feel confident that their website does a great job of clearly explaining what they do while also helping to connect visitors with their brand and people in a meaningful way.

Video can play a key role in addressing these challenges on your digital properties, helping you boost both engagement and conversion rates on your website and landing pages.

While some of these videos may warrant partnering with an agency, many can (and should) be created in-house with your own employees. That's the best way to showcase your passion, knowledge, and the "why" behind what you do.

Some key videos that will help you deliver a more insightful and delightful website experience include:

- Explainer videos for your business and your main products or services
- Deep-dive videos that clearly demonstrate what you offer and how it all works
- Transparent pricing videos (as Marcus previously mentioned) that answer the question *everyone* wants answered
- Landing page videos to increase conversion rates on form submissions and sign-ups

Now, we'll dive into each of these video types individually in the chapters that follow.

Chapter 35

HOW TO EXPLAIN WHAT YOU DO IN A CLEAR, CONCISE, AND MEMORABLE WAY ON YOUR WEBSITE

Have you ever gone to a vendor's website, read through their home-page and main solution pages, and still struggled to clearly understand exactly what problems they solve? Or have you ever felt frustrated by having to read numerous paragraphs and dozens of bullet points to learn the basics of what they do, all the while knowing that a short video would have been much more helpful and faster to consume?

Have you ever wanted to shout, *"Just **show** me already!"* at your monitor, out loud? Me, too.

And that's exactly why *explainer* videos are becoming more common across business websites. It's the simple idea of publishing short videos on your homepage and key pages across your website to clearly and concisely tell your story and to explain ideas that may seem simple to you but are likely very complex for your prospects.

After all, if a picture is worth a thousand words, a two-minute explainer is worth 3.6 million words. (Yes, I did the math on that one!) Having effective explainers at key points throughout your website can lead to a number of benefits for both you and your site visitors.

For your site visitors, explainer videos offer a more efficient and effective way to learn about you. They're easier to process, simpler to visualize, and a more efficient use of their time. Prospects can often learn more from a two-minute video than they can from reading text for 10 minutes or more.

This type of video also delivers your story in a format that is more clear, more memorable, and more relatable for your audience.

Using an effective story arc in video format can make it much easier for them to relate to the problem, identify with the main character, and connect the dots between what the challenge is and how your solution can help to solve it. For many site visitors, one or more explainer videos may just be the perfect way to lean back and soak it all in.

Now, for your marketing and sales teams, explainer videos can be powerful tools for converting prospects and accelerating the buyer's journey.

First, they can help you increase your average time-on-page because those visitors who choose to watch the video are more likely to stay on your site for two minutes or more, as opposed to those who simply skim your text content quickly and move on. From a digital marketing and SEO perspective, this is an important signal to search engines that your content is of high quality and relevance and, therefore, can help with your domain authority and search rankings.

Second, it's simply the fastest and most effective way to educate site visitors, create a sense of urgency, and stimulate demand for your solution.

Finally, explainer videos can be repurposed in a number of ways to help you generate demand beyond just your website. They may be an effective addition to your email marketing and nurturing programs. They might also perform well on your YouTube channel as a transition from thought leadership to learning more about what you do. They can also be effective in the hands of your sales team for outbound prospecting and deal acceleration.

The typical formula for explainer videos is to create a two-minute animated explainer for your homepage to quickly introduce what you do.

However, given the growing appetite for video and increasing demand for genuine and authentic content, the opportunity for explainers goes well beyond this today. Explainers can be animated or live-action, and can be used on your homepage, product or service overview pages, key landing pages, and, frankly, on any page where you are trying to explain a relatively complex topic or where visitors may have questions that could be easily answered by a short video.

You don't need to add an explainer to every page on your site. However, I strongly encourage you to navigate through each of the main sections of your own website, asking yourself whether a video could help to more clearly tell your story, explain an idea, or answer a question your site visitor likely has at that moment in time.

Even if the question is simply, *"Is it really worth it to fill out that form?"*

There is no shortage of examples online for business explainer videos. A quick search will reveal lots of ideas to pull from—or head over to Vidyard's Video Inspiration Hub for a library of examples. You can also browse Vidyard's own website (**www.vidyard.com**) where we have a homepage explainer, solution-level explainer videos, and a myriad of examples throughout.

But if you're looking for something a little different—something that could make a B2B company really stand out—look no further than the teams at NetMotion Software and Uberflip.

NetMotion Software sent their product into space aboard a custom-made weather balloon to clearly explain what they offer in a way they simply couldn't with the written word.

Then there's Uberflip's explainer video series called 'ELI5' which is truly a work of art that will leave you laughing and curious to learn more.

Chapter 36

UBERFLIP'S EXPLAINER LEAVES YOU LAUGHING AND CRAVING MORE

"ELI5."

No, that's not the latest Star Wars droid or the lead character in *Short Circuit 2*. (Yes, that's the one where Johnny Five dresses up like a cowboy.) Rather, it's an acronym frequently used on the internet when someone doesn't understand a topic and is looking for a simple and clear explanation.

It stands for the simple idea of explaining an idea simply—*"explain it like I'm five-years-old."*

The team at Uberflip had this exact concept on their minds when planning out their new product explainer series with their agency partner OneMethod.

You see, Uberflip sells a content experience platform that helps marketing teams create highly engaging content experiences on their website. But the challenge is that this is a very new category of software and most businesses don't yet know what it is, or why they might need it. So, the Uberflip team was on the hunt for a fresh new approach to tell their story in a way that was clear, simple, and relatable, and leveraged the power of video to connect with their audience in a more personal way.

Not only did they land on a concept that made it easy for anyone to understand what they do, they also brought the idea of ELI5 to life in the most **literal** sense.

At the time of writing this book, when you visit Uberflip's website at **www.uberflip.com** you're greeted by a lovely pink and white call-to-action button that says, "What We Do."

Once you press play, you're pulled into an entertaining skit involving two friendly and approachable people speaking to each other in an office. The video begins with a clever hook that makes its humorous and light tone immediately apparent; you can't help but think this one will be worth the watch.

The first person in the skit is an expert on Uberflip while the second is much like yourself—a business professional who doesn't know the first thing about Uberflip, nor why she might need a "content experience" platform.

When she casually asks the expert what Uberflip does, he launches into a well-rehearsed pitch filled with lots of big words and industry jargon. Taken aback, she responds, "Whoa, slow down there, Sheldon! Can you explain it to me like I'm a five-year-old?"

(Fans of *The Big Bang Theory* will appreciate the Sheldon reference!)

This kicks off a series of highly entertaining segments wherein the expert explains Uberflip like he's an entertainer at a children's birthday party, a dungeon master, and even as if he were her boss.

The pacing is pitch-perfect, the acting is terrific, and the humor is spot-on. So, not only does this explainer do its primary job of helping you understand what Uberflip does, it also leaves you laughing, curious, and genuinely craving more.

But don't worry, there are three more explainers in the series to satiate your appetite!

In the following segments the expert goes on to explain each of their main products like he's a baseball coach (think *Moneyball* analytics), a dad packing lunches for his kids (I can 100% relate to this analogy of every kid wanting a customized lunch), and, my personal favorite, like he's on the television show *The Bachelor*.

I'll stop trying to describe the videos here because words simply can't do them justice.

I spent some time interviewing the teams at Uberflip and OneMethod to better understand how this unique explainer series came to be. There were countless lessons learned along the way, but a few takeaways that really stood out for me included the following:

1. When trying to explain what you do, a fresh set of eyes can make all the difference.

In fact, during the process of revamping their explainers, Uberflip had scripted and recorded another version that, ultimately, got scrapped.

This first version was scripted by their own team who, by their own admission, realized they were too close to their own products, which made it exceedingly difficult to get away from industry terms and "product speak."

They then partnered with OneMethod, which had no experience at all with Uberflip. So, their team was forced to learn what they did **and** how to explain what they do with an outsider's point of view. Randy Frisch, Uberflip's CMO, noted that while it was initially difficult to take a step back and allow an outside team to try and explain what you do, it resulted in a much better final product that is accessible to a much broader audience.

2. Business people are people first.

The team at OneMethod typically does creative work for large consumer brands such as Burger King, Nestle, and Nike. The majority of their content in this world is story-driven, inspiring, humorous, and eye-catching—things that people naturally gravitate toward.

These ideas are common when producing promotions for large consumer brands but often forgotten in the broader world of business content. But, as OneMethod copywriter Mitch Robertson noted, business people are still people first! Like consumers, they want to be educated but they also want to be entertained. And the best way to keep them engaged for two minutes or longer is to deliver your message in a story-driven format that is interesting, entertaining, and highly relatable.

3. When you nail the four Es, you end up with something special.

These explainers are a great example of content in the broader business world that nailed all of the four Es of video—something difficult to do within a single piece of content. As a result, they stick with you and create an impulse to continue learning more.

Do yourself a favor and head on over to Uberflip's website, click that play button, and see for yourself. And, if you want to learn more of the backstory behind how these videos came to life, as well as what other lessons they learned along the way, check out my **Creating Connections** video and podcast series available on the Vidyard YouTube channel and your podcast provider of choice. Just look for the episode entitled "Video in Focus: Explain it Like I'm 5—Behind the Lens of the Top Explainer of 2019."

Chapter 37

HOW TO USE DEEP-DIVE VIDEOS TO CREATE A FRICTION-FREE WEBSITE EXPERIENCE

Explainer videos give site visitors the critical information they need as quickly as possible to make a decision on whether or not they should proceed with learning more about your solution. Therefore, they are usually kept high-level in their messaging and no longer than two or three minutes in length.

But once someone has seen enough to determine they're interested in what you do, they will now be willing to invest more time to learn about what you offer. A big mistake that many companies make at this stage is equating that *willingness to invest more time with a willingness to speak with a sales rep.*

That's why conversion rates on that next big call-to-action on most websites—"request a demo" or "book a meeting"—are typically very low.

Some argue that this is totally OK; they're willing to lose out on some opportunities in favor of getting contact details for hot leads who may be ready to buy. I would argue, however, that this is a huge missed opportunity, and that countless potential buyers are slipping through the cracks because they are interested in what you do, but not yet interested in speaking with sales.

There's an easy way to combat this in a way that capitalizes on a potential buyer's immediate interest in learning more but does not present the same level of friction as having to book a call with a sales rep.

Offer up a new call-to-action on your website that says "**watch a demo**," "**see** for yourself," "**take** a tour," or "**see** our services in action."

In essence, you're offering them a self-service, on-demand video experience to see your products or services in action. How novel and refreshing!

However, most companies still choose to keep these options hidden, forcing prospects to speak with sales to learn more. They'll justify the need to involve a sales rep in these moments in various ways.

"We need to customize our demos to their unique needs," or *"We don't want our competitors seeing it."*

At face value, these may sound like logical objections. But the reality for most is that this is really just a sales tactic.

The price of admission to see the good stuff is to give us your information and to get you on a call with a sales rep—because once you do, you're more likely to convert (and if you don't, we've got your phone number forever!). Yes, that approach may have worked in years past, but those days are quickly coming to an end and businesses need to adapt.

So, put yourself in the shoes of one of your prospects and go through your own website to understand the experience for yourself. Think critically about what the next step in your own friction-free buying journey should be if the dreaded sales meeting were no longer an option.

If you're worried about the risk of losing out on the opportunity to get their email address and phone number, don't. Your focus should be on making the content so valuable that they would be silly not to contact you after watching. Or consider making it so irresistible that a submission form seems like a small price to pay to unlock the content—especially if it means they don't need to hop on the phone.

One of the best examples of this is how the team at Marketo has radically increased conversion rates on their website, while also reducing the average time to qualify a new visitor through the strategic use of on-demand, video-based demonstrations.

Chapter 38

MARKETO INCREASES WEBSITE CONVERSIONS BY 1,103% WITH VIDEO

Marketo's website (**www.marketo.com**) is one of my favorite examples of a conversion-centric website done well, as it should be!

After all, Marketo (now an Adobe company) is a leading provider of solutions for marketing automation, customer engagement, and digital marketing experiences. Their products are designed to help marketers optimize engagement and conversion, and their own practices have long been a strong reflection of that.

A few years ago, Marketo began experimenting more heavily with video content. This initially led to the creation of more video-based resources for their website, visual thought leadership content, and promotional videos to support their events.

But perhaps the most impactful video experience they've built to date is the "4-Minute Demo" on their website.

The experience is quite brilliant in its simplicity. At the time of writing this book, as you navigate around Marketo's website, two main calls-to-action follow you around on virtually every page: "Request a Demo" and "Watch a 4-Minute Demo." In fact, these are not only placed strategically in the website header and across key pages, they're also prominently displayed within the navigation bar and via a "sticky footer" that remains, well, "sticky" at the bottom of each page as you scroll.

The marketer in me immediately appreciates that these are the next-step actions that Marketo really wants me to take. And what shouldn't come as a surprise is that "Watch a 4-Minute Demo" quickly became the highest converting call-to-action—by a long shot.

> *"At first, video was just a hunch. We suspected it'd help us attract attention, so we A/B tested how visitors converted when they saw our regular home page versus a four-minute demo. The demo increased conversions by a number that seems unbelievable: **1,103%**.*
>
> *The question is: Why?*
>
> *I have some guesses. Time-starved buyers now expect explainer and demonstration videos to help them cut to the chase. They arrive on a site with questions such as, 'What does this company do? Is this for me? How can they help?' and want those answers quickly. They aren't interested in speaking with sales until they clearly understand what we offer. On-demand demo videos save them from browsing and reduces cognitive effort."*
>
> ***Paulo Martins, Global Head of Commercial Digital Marketing, Marketo and Adobe Experience Cloud***

Creating more clicks is nice, but the real magic is what happens next.

Once you select "Watch a 4-Minute Demo," you're taken to a landing page to complete a form prior to unlocking the demo.

This is the new lead generation part of the experience, which may be important if people are selecting this instead of booking a meeting. After all, you need to keep that sales team busy! But are people really willing to fill out a form to watch a video? Yes!

Especially if you position it as something like a "4-Minute Demo." Four minutes sounds like enough value to make it worth my while (it's deeper than a two-minute explainer), but not so much that I'm going to have to sit through a long, boring product pitch. *Sold!*

Then, once you complete the form, you're not just taken to a page with a single four-minute demo. It's so much more! You're brought into a Netflix-style experience where you can binge on multiple four-minute demos—one for each main product offering, as well as a comprehensive 25-minute product walkthrough, should the mood strike you.

But the fun doesn't stop there!

As a lead starts watching the demo content, every second of engagement is tracked by their video hosting platform, Vidyard, and pushed into their lead record in marketing automation. So, if you choose to watch two minutes of the email marketing demo, only 30 seconds of the marketing automation demo, and all four minutes of the account-based marketing (ABM) demo, all of that is tracked for lead qualification.

Highly engaged leads are then pushed to the sales team for immediate follow-up, and the insights on what they chose to watch (and skip) help them reach out with a more personalized message—in this case, it would focus on ABM as that is clearly an area of interest.

This approach is genuinely a win-win situation.

For the website visitor, it offers a self-service experience where they can learn about their products at their leisure in an on-demand environment. For Marketo, it drives more engagement on their website, creates well-educated prospects, and enables their sales team to focus solely on those leads who are showing the greatest level of interest.

Not only has this increased conversion rates on their website by more than 1,000%, it has also helped them convert new leads on their website from an "inquiry" to a marketing qualified lead (MQL) six times faster. So, it should come as no surprise that when you click on that *other* main website button that says "Request a Demo" you're taken to the exact same landing page to unlock the video demos.

Try it for yourself, then consider what *your* main video-based call-to-action should be. And remember, imitation is the greatest form of flattery.

Chapter 39

HOW TO JUSTIFY YOUR COSTS AND EARN TRUST WITH TRANSPARENT PRICING VIDEOS

Once a website visitor has learned the basics about what you do, where are they likely to head next? The "contact us" form? Your customer testimonials? Maybe your resource center?

Not likely.

The most common next step on the buyer's journey is to visit your pricing page. Like it or not, the natural instinct for new prospects is to learn about your pricing *before* they spend any more time learning about you.

And even though Marcus already explained this video from a sales perspective, it's too important not to further analyze this subject from the marketing side of things as well.

If you think about it, it totally makes sense. If your pricing model isn't aligned with their expectations or budgets, they won't want to waste any more time digging through your content.

It's just like when you're retail shopping and you see that *amazing* coat in the window. What do you do before sifting through the display rack to find your color and size? You check the price to see if it's even in your ballpark.

If you realize it's way out of your price range, you immediately move on. But if the pricing is in-line with your expectations—or if someone quickly convinces you that it's worth the ticketed price—you spend the next 30 minutes trying on different sizes, checking online reviews on your phone, and convincing yourself you'd be foolish not to buy it.

So, as you can imagine, your pricing page may be one of the most important pages on your website. The copy on this page is like the tag on that beautiful coat, offering descriptive information about the cost and benefits.

But what about that friendly face? That personable individual who provides the context you need to understand why the cost is what it is, how that compares to other products in the market, and why it's worth that *and more?*

That's where video comes in.

A video on your pricing page adds that critical human touch to the pricing conversation.

It doesn't need to explain every nook and cranny of your pricing model, but it gives you an opportunity to explain your value at this critical moment in a very personal and trustworthy way.

Specifically, a video on cost and pricing should do three things:

1. Address all of the factors that drive the cost of your product or service up or down.

2. Discuss the marketplace in an open and honest way—why comparable products or services are cheaper or more expensive, and so on.

3. Talk about your product or service and why it costs what it costs; i.e. your value proposition.

This is no different from how a retail store employee would handle a pricing conversation in a live selling environment.

Going back to the previous example, they would earn your trust by explaining what features make certain coats more expensive than others, how the coat you're interested in compares to others in the market, and what makes this specific coat just right for you.

By delivering this type of information in video format, you have the ability to overcome communication gaps that occur when a salesperson isn't able to discuss a product or service directly with a buyer.

Pricing page videos are most effective when you have real individuals from your company explaining your pricing model in a natural, conversational, and honest tone. Minimize your use of industry jargon and acronyms, and be thorough and transparent in explaining how your pricing works.

Additionally, use visuals to your advantage to make your value proposition clear. For example, if you're explaining how your pricing compares to a competitive product that is cheaper but offers less value, use an image or video footage of your product or service in action to clearly show the additional value.

Seeing is believing.

Chapter 40

HOW TO MAXIMIZE LANDING PAGE CONVERSIONS WITH OBJECTION HANDLERS

Landing pages are another key element of modern websites and digital marketing programs—they're how your website visitors convert themselves into leads.

For the purposes of this discussion, a landing page can be thought of as any page on your website that has a data collection form on it that someone can fill out and submit, such as "get a quote," "book a meeting," "download the guide," or "watch the video series."

Let's be honest. Whenever we're faced with filling out a form on a website we haven't visited before, there's always that moment of hesitation. On the one hand, we want whatever it is that they're offering, right?

On the other hand, we've all been burned by a company (or three) on the internet before. So, understandably, we have some lingering trust issues that make us skeptical:

"Will this company sell or otherwise abuse my personal information, compromising my privacy?"

"Will they spam me with tons of emails I don't want?"

"Will their sales reps start blowing up my phone with unwanted solicitations?"

"What exactly is going to happen after I fill out the form, anyway—is what I'm going to get even worth it?"

A great way to earn that trust is to address these concerns head-on by providing authentic content that proactively answers these questions. What better way to deliver a message like this than with a short, personal video?

For example, if your landing page includes a form to download a PDF guide that was written by your content marketer Jesse, you can add a video next to the form with Jesse—yep, the *real* Jesse!—saying something like the following:

> *"Hey there! It's Jesse here. I'm the one who wrote this guide you're about to download!*
>
> *It's packed full of new ideas based on the latest research that our team has done, and I really hope you find it valuable.*
>
> *But you may be wondering, is it really worth filling out this form to get the goods? Are we just going to spam you with emails and phone calls after you download the guide?*

Don't worry, I get it. So, here's exactly what you can expect to happen once you hit submit . . ."

A video like this will not only help to alleviate the fears your site visitor may be feeling, it can also actually make them feel more connected to your people and brand—and even more interested in submitting the form to download the guide.

When adding this video to the page, put a very visible title near the video that says something to the effect of, "See exactly what will happen if you fill out this form."

Why that title? Because that's exactly what the visitor is wondering. And, truthfully, if you were to read a video title like that on a website, wouldn't you at least be curious to watch it? Frankness and transparency can be very refreshing for today's buyers, and a short, authentic video like this can be the perfect way to achieve it.

"But does this style of video actually increase conversions enough to justify the effort of creating them?"

You bet it does.

Marketers will see an average conversion lift of 80% for any landing page where they follow this approach. In fact, we've seen many cases where the number of people who filled out the form increased by as much as 150%! Think about the type of impact that could have on your business, whether you offer forms to download a guide, get a quote, or book a sales meeting?

Of course, to generate the best possible results, keep these videos as short as possible, while still clearly addressing the likely concerns your site visitor may have. Let them know exactly what will happen next, as well as how and **when** it will happen.

For example, on a contact us form, don't just say, "Someone will be in touch soon." Be more specific:

"Our sales team is really excited to speak with you; you will hear from one of us within 24 to 48 hours."

If possible, also explain why you are asking for this information, and how it will help to ensure that you can deliver them the most relevant and valuable experience going forward.

Finally, place this video prominently on the landing page and *encourage* your visitors to watch. Don't treat this video as a last resort to convert people who are about to bounce. Rather, it should be featured prominently as the delightful, human centerpiece of your landing page.

Not only will the video help you increase conversion rates on the landing page form itself, but you may also find that people who choose to watch the video will also be more likely to engage further with your brand or answer the phone when you do make the call.

Behold, the power of video.

Chapter 41

WEBSITE VIDEO CHECKLIST

Video content is the perfect way to create an insightful and delightful website experience that converts more visitors while humanizing your brand.

The following checklist outlines the most critical, battle-tested best practices on how to use video content to keep your visitors engaged and to maximize conversion rates on your website and landing pages:

☐ **Use explainers to describe the problems you solve in a clear and memorable way**

Explainer videos are the perfect way to educate website visitors on the problems you solve and how you do it. They can be animated or live-action, and are typically one to two minutes in length. Use narrative story arcs to lead the visitor from the problem they have to the solution you offer, and use the visual nature of video to make your message clear, memorable and authentic.

☐ **Use deep-dive videos to showcase what you do and how you do it**
People come to your website for a very specific reason—to learn about what you do! Stop hiding behind the "contact sales" button and give your site visitors deep-dive videos that show your product in action and go behind-the-scenes of how you deliver your services. Give them an on-demand, self-service experience to answer all the questions they may have. Consider adding a gated form before or after key assets for new lead generation.

☐ **Add a short video to your pricing page to create clarity and trust**
On many business websites, the pricing page is one of the most frequently visited pages across their entire site. Use video on this page as an opportunity to clearly explain how your pricing works and what value specific customers get in return. Having a real executive or employee from your company explaining your pricing will also instill a sense of trust and transparency at this critical point in the buying journey.

☐ **Use short videos to increase landing page conversion rates**
Add a short video to landing pages that include a critical form or call-to-action to help you increase conversion rates. Feature one of your own employees clearly explaining the benefit in taking the next step, as well as what to expect after filling out the form. Directly address any concerns or hesitations that your visitor may have at that important moment.

Chapter 42

HOW TO BREATHE NEW LIFE INTO YOUR EMAIL MARKETING AND NURTURING SEQUENCES

Once someone has identified themselves on your website and opted in for communications, a common next step is to enroll them in some form of automated email marketing program.

The most common goals of email marketing are to maintain engagement and increase brand awareness with known prospects, to continue to educate potential buyers and generate demand for your solution over time, and to promote new or important campaigns that are designed to re-engage cold prospects.

For some, email marketing manifests itself as one-off communications when new content or campaigns are ready to be shared. For others, it may include thoughtfully-planned email nurturing workflows that automate the delivery of personalized content over time, based on a set of dynamic rules and filters—when someone last visited your website, engagement with particular topics of content, a time-bound drip campaign, and so on.

No matter how you approach email marketing, it's probably fair to say that it feels harder than ever to get these audiences to pay attention to your emails.

Most people are now ignoring anything that looks like unwanted spam, a sales pitch, or marketing collateral. It's kind of like when you go to the mailbox, and you toss anything and everything that looks like "junk mail," and, ultimately, sighing to yourself when you're left with a stack of bills and maybe a letter from your Aunt Sally.

Everything else—all of those bright and colorful printed ads, post-cards, and mailers from brands—goes right in the trash bin.

As a result, the best way to use email in today's business world is to share interesting and relevant content that people genuinely find value in and to build a relationship over time such that when they are ready to evaluate a solution within your space, you're the first one they call.

But in practice, most emails sent by brands today are what I like to call the "black and blue messages" of the automation era. Because email has always been associated with text-based content, these messages are almost always an uninspiring, ho-hum block of black text and blue hyperlinks with snooze-worthy calls-to-action that start with words like "download" and "schedule."

While the black and blue messages may have their place, you're potentially missing a huge opportunity to leverage email as a direct channel through which you can share any type of content including imagery, podcasts, interviews, and of course, videos.

Chapter 43

HOW TO THINK OUTSIDE THE INBOX WITH CREATIVE VIDEO IN EMAIL MARKETING

Let's pretend for a moment that you're crafting an automated email that is intended to promote a new research report you've published. Or perhaps a blog post on a "hot topic du jour."

The main call-to-action in the email could be a link to "Download the Report" or "Read the Article." Or you could take a more exciting route with something like "Watch the 1-Minute Summary."

Which would your audience members be more likely to act on? In some cases, "Download the Report" may outperform, but in many cases

"Watch the 1-Minute Summary" will better resonate with today's audiences and feel like a more efficient use of their time.

After watching the one-minute video, they will likely feel as if they received some great value that respects their time and attention, and they can easily dive into the full report as a next step after the video. As an added bonus, if the video features someone from your business clearly explaining the key takeaways, it also becomes an opportunity to establish a personal connection between buyer and seller and to earn more trust along the way!

This is just one of many examples of how you can use video-based calls-to-action within email marketing to increase your click-through, engagement, and downstream conversion rates.

When it comes to using video content in your automated emails, a great place to start is to identify existing videos you have that align with your email marketing or nurture strategy.

Begin by focusing on thought leadership videos that are designed to educate your audience and offer unique value, without feeling like you're trying to sell to them. If you've created relevant thought leadership videos for your YouTube channel, social media, or blog, start repurposing those within your email marketing program.

Then, use a creative subject line that includes the word "video" to pique their interest, include some short introductory copy that includes words like "short," "2-minute," or "exclusive" to make the content feel even more irresistible. Also, add a thumbnail image for your video with a nice big play button on it that takes them to a landing page to immediately watch!

The goal of these emails is not to get someone to immediately contact your sales team, but to re-engage with your brand and to educate them on the path to long-term conversion. For some viewers, your helpful video will remind them that they need help solving the problem you address—so, make sure that button to contact sales (or to watch an online demo!) is always nearby.

Much like with your social video strategy, the next step to your visual email experience is to create new video assets designed explicitly for your email marketing and nurture programs.

Unlike social media, your email audience should already be familiar with your brand and is likely further on in the buyer's journey, affording you the opportunity to use longer-form content as well as videos that start to explain what you do, how you do it, and how you have helped others produce big results.

Although social media is inherently defined by one-to-many com-munications, email marketing allows you to be more targeted by creating recipient lists based on their company size, industry, job title, and even their previous content consumption behaviors.

This level of segmentation allows you to get much more specific and personalized in the video content you share.

Videos that tend to work well in automated email marketing and nur-turing programs include:

- **High-level thought leadership videos** with broad appeal to your overall audience, often used during the early stages of automated email nurtures and for a broad segment of your list.

- **Targeted thought leadership videos** with specific appeal to subsegments of your audience, typically used during mid-stages of automated email nurtures and for more narrow segments of your list.

- **Customer journey videos** that showcase how you've helped other businesses or consumers solve problems or meet their goals, often used in later stages of automated email nurtures.

- **Product or service overview videos and online demonstrations** to encourage your audience members to self-educate on your products or services, often used in later stages of automated email nurturing campaigns.
- **Custom videos to support specific offers,** campaigns, product or service launches, content asset launches, and more, often sent out in a timely manner to support key priorities and initiatives.

Chapter 44

HOW TO MAXIMIZE ENGAGEMENT WITH THE RIGHT SUBJECT LINE AND THUMBNAIL IMAGE

Once you've identified the video content your email subscribers will fall absolutely *head over heels* for, the next step is to incorporate them into automated emails in a way that will maximize your engagement rate.

The three key email marketing metrics you'll want to watch are:

1. **Click-to-open rate (CTOR),** or the percentage of people who open the email, which is heavily dependent on the subject line and preview copy.

2. **Click-through rate (CTR)**, or the percentage of people who click through on the main link or call-to-action in the email, which is heavily dependent on what the offer is and how it's positioned.

3. **Post-click engagement rate or conversion rate,** or the percentage of people who actively engaged in the content or submission form linked to from the email. You know, the *real* action you were trying to drive from the email.

The thing I love about using video in email marketing is that it's no one-trick pony.

When you use video in your emails effectively, you can impact each of these key metrics for a big net effect on your success. All it takes is a bit of creativity, a willingness to test and experiment, and following a few of the video-in-email best practices below.

The best way to increase your **click-to-open rate** is to use a creative subject line that catches people's attention and creates a sense of curiosity.

For emails that include a video as a call-to-action, try adding the word "video" somewhere in the subject line. The latest research suggests that emails with "video" in the subject line generate a 19% higher open rate than those that don't. You can do this by weaving the word organically into the subject itself or by adding [Video] at the beginning or end of the subject line. Get creative, have fun with it, and be sure to test different variants to see what works best for *your* business.

To maximize your **click-through rate** on the link to the video itself, there are a number of things to be mindful of.

First, start the email with some short copy to set the necessary context for the video. Pique their interest with some of our favorite tactics—pose a big question, challenge conventional wisdom—something that tees up your video as something that simply can't be missed.

Whatever you do, keep your introduction short and *let the video do the talking*.

Second, include a big, beautiful thumbnail image for the video immediately after your enticing introduction with a play button smack in the middle.

Visuals like this will draw their attention and the play button will make it clear that there's a great video to watch. Step things up by using an animated GIF image for your thumbnail that loops every three seconds! An animated thumbnail will draw more attention because of the visual movement and will often demand a higher click-through rate as a result.

Third, hyperlink the image to the landing page with your video—videos can't be natively embedded in emails, so you need to link out to a webpage with the video. But you should also offer a direct link to the video within the email copy before or after the thumbnail image.

Use phrases like "Watch the 2-minute video" or "See for yourself" to quickly turn readers into viewers.

Last, but certainly not least, to maximize **post-click engagement** and **conversion rates**, be mindful of the experience your viewer will have when landing on the destination webpage.

If you are using YouTube to host your video, one option is to link out directly to the YouTube page for that video. While this is an easy option, it's not an ideal experience for your viewer or for your brand given the number of distractions on YouTube—like those darn cat videos and movie trailers!—and the lack of control you have in offering additional content or next-step conversions.

With YouTube, you also lose the ability to track whether or not that individual clicked play or acted on any additional links or calls-to-action you may have included.

Instead, host your video on a dedicated landing page using either your web content management system (CMS) or your video hosting platform, and link to that page from within the email.

When using a more advanced video hosting solution than YouTube, each video you upload can have its own dedicated landing page that is custom-branded for your business *and* free of ads and distractions. In turn, this allows you to slide a direct link to your video as a call-to-action in your email, like the smooth operator you are.

Alternatively, you can add your video to a custom landing page created with your web CMS, which gives you even more control over the layout and branding of the page, as well as what types of additional content and offers you include below the video.

Finally, if you are using a business-grade video platform like Vidyard you can not only track who clicked play on the video, but you can also see how long they engaged with the content. That's a big deal because you can then use those insights within your marketing and CRM tools to identify, qualify, and reconnect with your most engaged prospects.

Chapter 45

VIDEO IN EMAIL MARKETING CHECKLIST

No matter what types of videos you share in your email marketing, always think about how they could be leveraged to advance your goals of increasing your email open, click-through, engagement, and conversion rates.

To help guide you, here are the most important best practices you need to know to guarantee you get the most out of every email with video:

☐ **[Video] Get creative and smart with your subject line**
Make it clear in your subject line that an amazing video awaits them within this email message. Use the word "video" or "watch" within the subject line or try adding [Video] at the beginning or end. Split test different variants if possible to see what works best for your audience to maximize your click-to-open rate.

☐ **Tease out your video content but don't spoil the surprise.**
Include two to three short sentences of copy to set the context
for your video, but keep it short and direct. Use this copy
to capture their attention, to set the stage for the video, and
to create a sense of urgency to watch—but don't spoil the
key takeaways! Use terms like "short" or "1-minute" when
referencing the video or within the hyperlinked call-to-action to
maximize your click-through rate.

☐ **A thumbnail image is worth a thousand words**
While you can't embed videos directly within emails, you
can give your audience the next best thing! Include a large
thumbnail image for your video with a visible play button in
the middle to draw their attention and increase click-through
rates. Make it even more irresistible by using a looping
animated GIF instead of a static image to see if your click-
through rates improve even more.

☐ **"Watch this!" Don't forget to make the main CTA clear
and concise.** Ensure that the thumbnail image for the video
is hyperlinked to a page where the video is the hero, but
also be sure to include hyperlinked text or a button after
the thumbnail image as your final call-to-action. The text
or button can say something as simple as "Watch Now" or
"View the 1-Minute Video."

☐ **Link to an optimized destination page for your video**
When an email subscriber clicks on the hyperlink or the
thumbnail image, they're expecting to immediately watch your
video. So, link to a page where the video is prominent and can
be quickly watched—*don't* force them to scroll down a page or

search for it. This could be a link to the YouTube page for that video, the dedicated sharing page for that video created by your video hosting platform, or to a custom landing page on your website or resource center that features that video.

☐ **Consider having your video autoplay when viewers come from the email**
If your video is hosted on YouTube and you link directly to the page for that video, it will autoplay by default. If your video is hosted on a dedicated sharing or landing page, you can also configure it so the video will autoplay when the link in your email is selected. Depending on your video hosting platform, this may be configured as a default setting for the video itself, or you may be able to append a special value to the end of the link in the email such as "autoplay=true" to have the video autoplay when the page is loaded via this link.

☐ **Don't forget closed captions for those who prefer to read along**
Remember, people will be clicking through to your video as they're going through their email inbox and, just as with social media, they may not have been planning to sit down and watch videos with their headphones on. Closed captions enable your viewers to quickly watch the video with their sound turned off while also guaranteeing your content is accessible to the widest possible audience.

Chapter 46

HOW TO MAKE YOUR BIG CAMPAIGNS AND CONTENT INVESTMENTS COUNT WITH VIDEO

As a marketer myself, I love planning, executing, and optimizing the day-to-day tactics that help us continuously move the needle on website traffic, followers, qualified leads, and new sales opportunities. It's a highly satisfying blend of art and science that creates a well-oiled marketing machine that never stops running.

But what I love *even more* is creating the big campaigns that support new and exciting product launches, the release of major content assets, key lead generation activities, customer events, and more. For some marketing teams, big campaigns happen once or twice a year. For others, they happen every quarter or even every month.

Whatever your frequency is, creative video content can be the perfect way to ensure your biggest campaigns of the year stand out and have the greatest possible impact.

BOOST ENGAGEMENT IN PRODUCT OR SERVICE LAUNCHES BY TELLING A GREAT STORY

I've worked at a number of product companies supporting both B2C and B2B product launches.

If there's one thing I've learned the hard way through those experiences, it's how difficult it is to get prospects and customers to actually care about your new offerings. Let's face it, there's more at stake for *you* in the new launch than there is for *them*, right? *Wrong.*

The problem I've seen time and again is that businesses get caught up in the idea that they're launching a new product or service, as opposed to *solving a new problem for their customers.*

It's something that I came to truly appreciate more than 15 years ago during my time at BlackBerry (the original smartphone!) where every product enhancement, every new software feature and hardware optimization, was made through the lens of how it would help the customer be more productive. Every new phone and every new app wasn't just a new product, it was a solution to a problem that you absolutely needed to solve.

When you flip your thinking in that way, it becomes clear that there's just as much at stake for your customers as there is for your own business when you launch something new.

It may solve the problem of inefficiency, ineffectiveness, or inability to achieve a certain goal. It may be as small as making it easier to accomplish a common task or workflow, or as big as helping them accelerate revenue growth by 30%. Or perhaps you've launched a new service that will help consumers reduce debt and improve their long-term financial position.

Whatever it is, your goal is to tell that story. The story that brings their problem or pain point to life in a way that's relatable, emotional, and creates a sense of urgency to act.

How can you do that? With video.

To support your new product or service launch, think about how to tell a great story that focuses on the *problem* your new offering solves.

You can use scenario-based "skits" to bring that pain to life, have one of your own employees speaking to the viewer on camera explaining the problem directly, or capture one of your customers talking about the problem in a way that others can relate to.

Once you've showcased the problem and made it painfully clear to your viewer, offer a short teaser of your new product or service and a deep dive demo of how it actually works. This can all be done via a single video, but it often makes sense to create one promotional video to tee up the problem and a teaser of your solution, and then a second educational video that walks the viewer through the new offering (education) in a more comprehensive way.

Your prospect or customer should walk away after a few minutes of viewing with a clear understanding of why your new offering exists, what specific problem it solves, what it actually looks like, and how they could apply it within their own business or personal life.

It's a perfect execution of the four Es of video to drive greater demand and adoption for your new products and services.

MODERNIZE YOUR E-BOOKS, REPORTS, AND OTHER MAJOR CONTENT ASSETS

Many businesses are now creating high-value content assets such as e-books and research reports to support their inbound marketing, thought leadership, and lead generation programs.

If you're creating these already, you know your content is built to have broad appeal, and you're likely promoting them through various channels, like your website and blog, email marketing campaigns, social media, and maybe even a few paid third-party channels.

A great way to maximize the reach and impact of assets like these is to create short companion videos to complement and/or promote what you've created. These videos can help you drive more conversions to the core content asset and foster engagement with audience members who may not be ready to read the entire report but are still interested in seeing the big takeaways.

A great example of this is how the team here at Vidyard promotes our annual **Video in Business Benchmark Report**.

The report itself is more than 30 pages in length and published as a PDF document on our website. We share it directly with known customers and prospects, and also gate it behind a registration form for all other visitors to support our new lead generation efforts.

Like other key content assets, our Video in Business Benchmark Report is promoted via email marketing, social media, and on Vidyard's website with direct links to "Download the Report."

In addition to this, our marketing team creates short promotional videos to capture people's attention and drive awareness of the report. These short videos each highlight a key statistic or take-away from the report, acting as a teaser for the kinds of insights people can expect. (They're like short commercials to promote the main report.)

Another approach to maximizing the impact of major content assets is to create video content that acts as a companion to the written piece or to create a full video-based version of the hero content.

These videos can be relatively quick to produce because all of the primary messaging and the story arc have already been written for your hero asset. You can use that content to prepare a video version of the report or, alternatively, you could create a series of short videos, perhaps one video for each major chapter.

If identifying new leads is an important goal of your content, you can also gate the video(s) with a lead capture form and use second-by-second video viewing data to discover your most engaged leads to follow up with.

Chapter 47

GORDIAN DRIVES $6 MILLION WITH EDUCATIONAL VIDEO SERIES

If you Google "Glenn Hughes" you'll find no shortage of articles about the English rockstar who played bass guitar and performed vocals for bands like Deep Purple, Phenomena, and Black Sabbath.

He's a brilliant musician who helped to build the funk rock movement and was inducted into the Rock and Roll Hall of Fame in 2016. But in the world of content and video marketing, there's a different rockstar who creates his own timeless classics and has proven that you don't need big label budgets to produce a top 10 hit.

That man is also named Glenn Hughes, and he's the in-house video producer at Gordian.

Gordian is a leading provider of construction software, cost data, and procurement services for all phases of the construction lifecycle. They primarily service government agencies and local municipalities, as well as healthcare and education institutions.

When new construction projects are required by an organization in one of these markets, they turn to companies like Gordian to forecast project and material costs, identify potential builders and contractors, and manage the overall procurement process.

"WHAT IS JOB ORDER CONTRACTING?"

Within the world of construction, cost data and procurement is an important process known as job order contracting (JOC).

For purposes of this discussion, the details of JOC are unimportant, but what *is* important to know is that "What is Job Order Contracting?" is a commonly asked question by potential buyers in Gordian's market—and something they always want to be the ones to answer. Just like how here at Vidyard we want to be the ones to answer "What is a Video Marketing Platform?"

For your own business, there are undoubtedly similar questions that you want to be the authority on.

The team at Gordian had already invested the effort to create a variety of blog posts, e-books, and guides to answer this question, as part of their inbound marketing strategy. But as the new production lead, Glenn knew that video would be a more effective way to educate potential buyers about this complex, multi-faceted topic.

He also understood that, if they approached it in the right way, video could not only be used to attract new leads and generate awareness, but also to accelerate someone through the buyer's journey faster than any written content.

> *"Our goal in marketing is not just to generate marketing qualified leads (MQLs) but to also move the needle by guiding a prospect through the buyer's journey so we see the impact to our bottom line. We decided video would be the most useful media for achieving that goal. It allows us to humanize our brand, products, and stories and it provides us with detailed analytics for tracking engagement,"*
>
> **Glenn Hughes, *video producer at Gordian***

In the summer of 2018, Glenn and his marketing colleagues embarked on their first full-funnel video campaign called "Job Order Contracting 101."

Using a series of five videos, consisting of a one-minute teaser and four gated deep-dive videos, Gordian's campaign walks a potential lead through everything they need to know about job order contracting—what it is, how it works, when to use it (using social proof), and how to set up their own program.

Much of the content is similar to what had already been published in text-based blogs and guides, but video allowed them to bring this narrative to life in a more authentic, engaging, and memorable way.

$6 MILLION IN REVENUE IN 6 MONTHS

The end result was a four-part, 25-minute long video series that directly generated more than $20 million in qualified deals in their pipeline and $6 million in revenue within the first six months of release.

What?! Those are some very, very big numbers.

Are the videos really *that* incredible? Well, the videos themselves are good, yes. But the success of this campaign hinged on some other critical factors.

First, they **packaged and productized** the content in a very smart way to support their lead generation goals. Instead of just releasing all the videos as free assets on YouTube, they built a landing page on their website with a registration form to unlock this incredibly valuable four-part video series.

And when you say it like that, people absolutely *will* fill out a form to watch videos. In fact, this is no different from how they would release an e-book or research report as a new lead generation tool.

Second, they **promoted the video series** in a number of different ways. They shared promotional assets for organic social media, paid advertising, email marketing, and more. They produced a one-minute promotional teaser video and published it on their YouTube channel with the title, "What is Job Order Contracting and How Does it Work?" This teaser video is now the top search result in Google under the "videos" tab when searching for "job order contracting."

At the end of the teaser video, viewers are directed to the landing page on Gordian's own website where they can fill out the form to unlock the full series.

Finally, they **used second-by-second video engagement data** to track, qualify, and convert their most engaged viewers into sales opportunities. They accomplished this using Vidyard's video hosting platform, integrated with their Marketo marketing automation and Salesforce CRM, to host and publish the videos.

As soon as someone completes their video viewing session, all of the details on which video(s) they watched and how long they engaged are pushed to their lead records in marketing automation where it can be actioned. Leads who watch for a short period of time are added to an automated email nurturing workflow, while those who watch longer are pushed to their sales team for immediate follow-up.

While e-books and guides offer visibility into who is downloading which content, videos provide the opportunity to track the actual engagement time with each topic, enabling them to prioritize follow-up with their most engaged leads. Their sales team absolutely loves this.

With the right planning and the right technology, Glenn and his rockstar team were able to take an in-house created video series from the top 100 charts to a No. 1 smash hit—and they now have a repeatable formula for generating more business through engaging visual content.

To check it out for yourself, search online for "Gordian Job Order Contracting 101" and let the inspiration soak in. Or watch Glenn explain his overall approach to video marketing on the **Video in Focus** show found on Vidyard's YouTube channel.

Rock on, Glenn! We'll see you soon in the Video Marketing Hall of Fame.

Chapter 48

HOW TO MAXIMIZE ENGAGEMENT IN KEY LEAD GENERATION CAMPAIGNS

Depending on the nature of your business, lead generation campaigns can take many different forms. You may be promoting a live event or your participation at a key industry conference. You could be driving registrations for an upcoming webinar you're hosting or launching a new advertising campaign designed to attract new leads.

Whatever the program may be, the goal of a lead generation campaign is to engage a targeted audience in your message and to convert as many of them as possible on the desired next step, such as clicking a link, completing a form, booking a meeting, or even buying now. These types of campaigns help marketing teams generate a spike in new qualified leads and/or accelerate demand from their existing prospect database.

While it may not be practical to create videos for every lead generation campaign you run, the effort can be well worth it for those campaigns where you're looking for a big return. Video can play a supporting role, helping you drive more interest in the key hero assets or message, or it can play a starring role where the video content itself is the main attraction.

For example, think about how you might approach driving registrations for an upcoming event or webinar you're hosting. There are a number of ways to promote an event like this to both new and existing audiences, including organic social media posts, outbound email marketing, relevant thought leadership content that drives to the event as a call-to-action, direct promotion on your own website, and advertising via third-party media.

Eye-catching video can support all of these channels, offering a unique way to show your audience what they'll learn (educate), to introduce the real people who will be sharing their insights (establish empathy), and to make your message truly memorable by delivering it in a more personal and creative way (engaging and emotional).

One of my favorite examples is how the team at Influitive, a leading provider of customer advocacy and community software, created a truly memorable video experience to drive registrations for their annual conference, Advocamp.

In addition to promoting the event via traditional content types and channels, they produced a series of short videos that brought the personality of the conference to life in a big way. Playing off the "camp" theme, the videos were filmed in a summer camp setting and featured a camp counselor named Buck, a fictitious character who ended up playing a key role on-site at the event as well.

Buck spoke directly to the viewer as if they were attending the camp, using highly relatable summer camp analogies to explain what they would learn.

The videos were not only laugh-out-loud funny (and therefore highly memorable and shareable), they also brought the theme and emotion of the event to life in ways other formats simply couldn't. They also took the video to the next level by using automated personalization to customize the video for more than 10,000 unique recipients. Each of their target attendees received an email with a creative video that was personalized just for them, featuring their own name on merit badges and other props throughout the story.

By sending a personalized video that literally made each viewer a part of the story, they increased their click-through rate on email promotions by more than 800%. Now consider how a big spike in your own outbound campaign conversion rate could make *you* a happy camper.

Chapter 49

LOYOLA UNIVERSITY MARYLAND EARNS ATTENTION AND SPIKES ENROLLMENT

High school students today have a wealth of options when it comes to universities. Just as employers compete to attract top talent and businesses compete to attract new leads, academic institutions like Loyola University Maryland compete to attract students.

High school students will often apply—and be admitted—to multiple universities, and they'll also wait until the very last moment to confirm their acceptance. Standing out from "the competition" as a school during this yield period is a huge task, and the results can have a significant impact on enrollment numbers and resulting revenue.

As a result, the outbound communications to accept and "convert" prospective students is one of the most important campaigns of the year for the Loyola's marketing team:

> *"Between the months of December, when a student first is accepted, to May 1, the National Candidates Reply Date, we have a comprehensive marketing strategy to continue the conversation and secure a student's final acceptance.*
>
> *We recognize we are competing with many strong institutions who are also marketing to the same students during that period. From the programs we offer to the cost of tuition and our location—it all matters. We must be better than our competition. We have to shine."*
>
> **Genna Mongillo, Director of Marketing and Communications for Undergraduate Admission at Loyola University Maryland**

TRANSFORMING THE ACCEPTANCE EXPERIENCE

Until two years ago, high school students received an acceptance letter and welcome package delivered by mail from Loyola notifying them of their admission status. That all changed, however, when the university implemented a new customer relationship management system (CRM).

Suddenly, they had the ability to digitally communicate word of admission to students in real-time. It also opened a *whole new world* of creative opportunities for the admission and marketing teams.

Right around the same time, Associate Vice President of Marketing and Communications Sharon Higgins returned from a higher education conference with a new tool for the marketing team to try. Sharon came across Vidyard at the conference and saw the power of personalized video for herself, recognizing that it was something that could help their marketing campaigns stand out from the crowd.

After a highly successful initial test of a personalized welcome video for new students, the marketing team landed on the idea of using this approach to support their critical admission communications campaign—that one big program that could make or break final student enrollment.

After brainstorming different ideas around what was most likely to convert, they landed on a creative concept that leveraged the power of video to deliver a truly engaging and memorable experience.

The video that was delivered to the email inbox of each prospective student had a personalized thumbnail image. The thumbnail was taken from a scene within the video itself, where the school's mascot, Iggy the Greyhound, is holding up a sign saying "Congratulations [NAME]," with the [NAME] portion dynamically personalized for each recipient.

Once clicked, the student is taken to a landing page to watch *their* personalized acceptance video, giving them a sneak peek of what to expect as a student at Loyola. Friendly faces congratulate them on being accepted to the school and excited students share their passion and what they love about the campus experience. Finally, they're taken to a pep rally where Iggy is holding up a sign welcoming them personally to the Loyola experience.

In less than one minute, the prospective student feels more connected to Loyola, more engaged in their unique story, and more certain that this is the right school for them.

A RECORD-BREAKING, "OUTRAGEOUSLY" SUCCESSFUL CAMPAIGN

The video was sent to just over 8,000 admitted students, but it didn't receive 8,000 views; it received *more than 15,000 views* from nearly 12,000 unique individuals, along with more than 4,000 reviews online!

Not only did prospective students choose to watch their video, but many decided to share it with others. These were stand-out results for their marketing team, helping them on the way to their highest yield of first-year enrolled students in recent history.

> *"The video was outrageously successful. We saw the highest click-through and engagement rates of any campaign we've run in recent years. Combined with the rest of our marketing content, we yielded our largest first-year class in recent history."*
>
> **Genna Mongillo, Director of Marketing and Communications for Undergraduate Admission at Loyola University Maryland**

I can confidently say that this type of response generally doesn't happen with a traditional text-based acceptance email.

So, whether you're attracting new students, employees, or marketing leads, consider how visual storytelling (personalized or not!) can help take your key outbound campaigns to the next level of engagement.

Chapter 50

VIDEO FOR KEY CAMPAIGNS AND CONTENT CHECKLIST

Whether you've got big news to share or are running a key lead generation campaign, video content can help you stand out and tell a bigger story.

The following checklist outlines the best practices you need to know to guarantee you get the most out of your key campaigns and launches with online video content:

☐ **Make your product or service launch truly resonate by bringing their pain to life**
Video is the perfect way to share why you're launching a new product or service and to show how it will help. Use video content to bring the problem you're solving to life, and to

show your customers exactly what it delivers in a clear and memorable way.

☐ **Use short videos to promote your major content assets**
If you're using major content assets like e-books, guides, or research reports to generate new leads, create short promotional videos to tease audiences with key takeaways, and to generate interest in downloading the full content piece.

☐ **Reinvent your e-books and guides as engaging and memorable videos**
You've already got the content mapped out, now, deliver it in a fresh new way to engage a broader audience! Translate your main e-books, guides, and reports into educational videos or multi-part video series that you can package and promote in different ways and even use for new lead generation activities.

☐ **Use creative storytelling to drive engagement in key lead generation programs**
Whether you're promoting an event, driving registrations for a webinar, advertising a new offer, or re-engaging your list of dormant prospects, use the power of video to tell a bigger story and to make your promotional content more educational, engaging, emotional, and empathetic.

Chapter 51

HOW TO SUPPORT THE BUYING DECISION WITH VISUAL CUSTOMER STORIES

No one wants to buy from a company that can't prove that they've helped someone else like them achieve great results. On the flip side of that, *everyone* wants to buy from the company that gets rave reviews from their customers.

And in today's world of on-demand content and self-service buying journeys, customer testimonials (or "peer validation") need to be readily available, easily discoverable, authentic, and (most of all) trustworthy.

Peer validation can come in many forms—more traditionally, online reviews, testimonial quotes, and written case studies. But in today's visual world, there's no better way to share the success and satisfaction of your happy customers than through video-based customer stories.

CREATING A MORE HUMAN, PERSONAL, AND EMOTIONAL CUSTOMER STORY

Video-based customer stories not only make your testimonials feel more trustworthy and authentic, but they also give you the opportunity to bring out the passion and emotion of your clients in a way that can get future customers truly excited.

While written case studies can help you educate prospects on the results your other clients have realized, a video-based customer story is a perfect way to infuse their message with real emotion and to make them more relatable as real people solving real problems. And, if you plan and capture your story in just the right way, your prospects will see themselves in your clients and will aspire to become your next great story.

When approaching a video-based customer testimonial project, all three stages of planning (pre-production), recording (production), and editing (post-production) are extremely important to walking away with a compelling story that captivates your audience.

While the same could be said for any video you create, it's especially true for customer testimonials because you don't have the opportunity to script the narrative or define the storyline prior to starting the project. You'll often need to capture more footage than you'll end up using, and (in many cases) the *real* story that you end up bringing to life may be different than what you had expected going in!

It's almost like filming your own mini-documentary film. And like any great documentary, the best visual customer stories help audiences relate to the problem your protagonist was facing, understand the approach they took, and the tangible results they saw, and—perhaps most importantly—connect with the individuals on camera (their peers) in a very personal and human way.

These are the key elements that turn a simple written testimonial into a powerful story that motivates and inspires.

When planning and producing your video-based customer story, be mindful of the following best practices for each stage of the production lifecycle:

- **Be smart and explicit about who you are going to interview.** The individuals you capture on camera will have a big part to play in building your story. Choose one or more individuals that will be *credible* to your audience, *believable* in the story they convey, and *capable* of communicating on camera in a clear and concise way.

- **Capture multiple perspectives whenever possible.** Plan to interview two or more people via separate interviews to capture multiple perspectives on the problem and solution. This will give you more flexibility in how you build out the story in post-production, and will also mitigate the risk of anyone individual not being great or comfortable on camera.

- **Do your research and plan your questions ahead of time.** Winging it rarely works when getting your customers on camera. Before you hit record, you will need to have a general understanding of the story they have to tell, and plan out your questions accordingly. Don't be afraid to go off-script and ask new questions as they come to mind, but go into your interviews prepared to ask the questions that are most likely to get those amazing sound bites.

- **Be thoughtful about where you film your customer story.** If possible, film your customer story in the location where the key results are ultimately realized. If you're filming individuals from a business, this will often be at *their* office or perhaps on location with their customers. If you're filming a consumer, this may be in a more public space, at a retail store, or even at their home. If filming on-site is cost or time prohibitive, consider filming that at an industry conference that you're both attending or get scrappy with recorded video calls.

- **Film with two different camera angles if possible.** Using two different cameras will allow you to make what are called "jump cuts" in post-production in a more natural and fluid way. It will also enable you to create a more interesting and dynamic visual style by using different angles on your subject throughout the video.

- **Good lighting and audio go a long way.** Use natural or directional lights to make your customers look great on camera! And as with any other video you produce, audio quality is just as important as video quality. Use a clip-on lavalier microphone if possible to capture their voices clearly and to mitigate any background noise.

- **Good post-production editing will make or break engagement in your content!** It's easy to create a 30-minute long customer testimonial video that gives your audience the full story, *but no one is going to watch it.*

The real magic is in how you edit your footage down to a fast-paced and engaging video that is no longer than three to four minutes. Distill your content down to its most essential parts and use "b-roll" content such as footage of their office or home and shots of your product in action to make your finished product dynamic and engaging.

Whether or not you have in-house video production capabilities within your business, you may want to consider partnering with an agency or a freelance producer for your top customer stories.

Professional producers and video production agencies often come with the experience and equipment needed to get the most out of your customers on camera and to turn their answers to your questions into a compelling and engaging story.

Chapter 52

HOW TO BRING YOUR CUSTOMER STORIES TO LIFE IN NEW AND CREATIVE WAYS

Customer testimonial videos are the perfect way to validate the claims you make in the market and to showcase the results you've helped your clients achieve. While they focus on your customers and the results they've seen, ultimately, they are about your brand and why others should choose to do business with you.

As such, they are most effectively used in the later stages of the buyer's journey with prospects who are actively looking for a solution and considering multiple vendors.

However, testimonial style videos aren't the only way to use customer stories to generate new business. The stories of your customers can be brought to life in other creative ways that are interesting, relatable, and shareable, *and* not at all about your products or your brand.

INVISION'S DESIGN DISRUPTORS

The marketing team at InVision, a leading provider of user experience (UX) design tools, was so inspired by their users that they produced a documentary film to peel back the real stories of companies who have disrupted their markets through transformative design and user experiences.

The result was **Design Disruptors**, a beautifully produced 70-minute documentary film that gives the design community a never-before-seen view into the design approaches of these visionary companies.

The film is not about InVision's products, and it's not meant to be a testimonial for InVision. Rather, it's about bringing these stories to life in a way that brings value to their audience of designers and celebrates their achievements.

Because these stories aren't promotional in nature, the film is not only highly shareable within the design community, it's also now used by education institutions as part of their curriculum for UX and design.

THERMOFISHER SCIENTIFIC'S KEEP SEEKING

ThermoFisher Scientific is a B2B company, but the end-users of their products are real people—*imagine that!* Many of them are scientists who use their products every day for research and discovery.

The marketing team at ThermoFisher understood that what binds this community together is not only the pursuit of progress and discovery, but also the reality that most days involve setbacks and failed experiments.

Tapping into these shared experiences, they produced an amazing video series called **Keep Seeking** to share the human stories of how real scientists cope with failure in their day-to-day lives.

The series featured no actors, no products, no big stats—just honest stories from real people about how they handle failure and stay motivated in the face of adversity.

Each video is less than two minutes in length, but in this short window you're pulled into emotional stories of amazing people that you can immediately relate to. It's a celebration of these unique individuals and their shared experiences—brought to you by the most trusted brand in scientific progress, ThermoFisher.

These types of stories are an incredible way to build brand affinity and to earn trust within your community, provided you stay disciplined in not making them promotional assets for your products or services.

This is due to the fact that their power is rooted in their authenticity and the unabashed celebration of members of your community, *not* your own company.

As such, these types of stories can be used at every stage of the buying journey, not just for validation during the decision stage.

They work well on social media and YouTube for generating awareness and attracting new followers. They can be used as part of your outbound email marketing and lead generation programs, as a way of connecting with your audience in more emotional ways, in addition to keeping your brand top of mind without feeling like you're always just trying to sell something.

On top of that, they can be used during the consideration and decision stages—not to show the results customers see from using your products, but rather as a means to validate how connected you are to your community of customers, as well as how well you understand the challenges they face.

Visual storytelling of this nature can go a long way in helping you earn trust and credibility, and making people genuinely want to do business with your brand.

Chapter 53

VISUAL CUSTOMER STORIES CHECKLIST

Every customer has a story to tell, and every story can help you sell! Refer to the checklist below for best practices on how to use video to bring your customer stories to life in a way that will help you win more hearts *and* close more deals:

☐ **Use the power of video to infuse your customer stories with emotion and empathy**
Video gives you the opportunity to turn your customer testimonials into powerful stories that connect on a more personal level. Use video to bring out the passion of your customers, to showcase their humanity, and to make their story so relatable that your prospects feel like they're looking in a mirror.

☐ **Planning is the most important stage of a visual customer story production**
Well before you press record, learn your customer's story and the specific problems you've helped them address. Prepare your questions ahead of time and identify at least two individuals to interview to get multiple perspectives on camera.

☐ **Filming and production is also the most important stage**
Make your customers feel, look, and sound like a star! Be prepared to have good lighting, clear audio, and two cameras for recording at different angles. If possible, do your interview recording at the location where the results have been realized (their office, home, etc.) or get scrappy by recording onsite at a conference or even via video chat.

☐ **And post-production editing is also the most important stage**
Post-production is where all the magic happens for your customer story. Identify the key answers and quotes that support the narrative you're trying to tell, and edit the video down to its essential parts. Use background music to help with pacing and b-roll footage to maintain visual interest. Aim for your finished product to be no more than three or four minutes in length.

☐ **Go beyond testimonials to make your customers truly relatable**
Testimonials are just one way to share your customer stories. Consider other opportunities to tell their stories in a way that is all about them as an individual or a business, and not at all about your brand or your products. Make your customers the true hero and your content will be more approachable and highly shareable.

PART VI

USING VIDEO
MARKETING IN THE
POST-SALE STAGE

Chapter 54

HOW TO USE VIDEO TO DRIVE ADOPTION AND TURN CUSTOMERS INTO FANS

For a moment, I want you to think about a significant purchase that you or your business has made in recent years.

Did you buy a new car? Did you tackle a massive home renovation? Maybe you embraced a new way of managing your personal (or company's) finances? Or perhaps you implemented a new piece of marketing or sales technology?

Whatever it was, reflect on the experience you've had with that vendor *since you became a customer.*

How have they engaged with you during that time? Do you now have a negative, indifferent, positive, or an ecstatic "Oh my goodness, I just *love* this company!" type of sentiment toward their brand and people?

As a result of those feelings, how likely would you be to do business with them again or to recommend them to others? And if you were to leave a review about their business online, what would you say in that review?

Now, think about your own customers and how *they* would react to a similar set of questions about your business.

Would you be satisfied with most having an "indifferent" or "positive" sentiment toward your brand and an industry average net promoter score (NPS), their inclination to recommend you to others? Or do you want to be that business that stands out from the crowd, has an industry-*best* NPS, and has raving fans for customers who would go out of their way to promote your brand to others?

If you choose door number two, then everyone in your business needs to play an active role in defining and supporting the customer experience. And the role of marketing can be so much more than just publishing collateral and hosting customer events.

Chapter 55

HOW TO ACCELERATE ONBOARDING AND USER ADOPTION

Whether you're a large enterprise with a dedicated customer marketing team or a small business with individuals who wear many hats, there are numerous ways to create a visual, video-based experiences that drive your desired customer behaviors at scale.

Creative and personalized customer communications can be used in a variety of ways to educate, improve the onboarding experience, increase adoption and utilization, and generate new expansion or cross-sell opportunities.

And, when done with the human touch, it can also help put a trust-building "face" to your brand and build a more personal relationship.

DELIVERING AN EXCEPTIONAL ONBOARDING AT SCALE TO CUSTOMERS BIG AND SMALL

When a new customer signs on, you may have an onboarding period where your product or service gets initiated and your new clients are trained on how to get started. Depending on the nature of your business, you may have dedicated account managers and a "one-to-one" onboarding experience, a self-serve knowledge base with on-demand customer support, or a mix of both.

No matter where you fit on that spectrum, on-demand video content created by your marketing and sales team can go a long way to ensuring that each and every customer, big or small, receives an engaging, approachable, and easy-to-follow onboarding experience that shows them you really do care.

The power of video at this stage of the customer lifecycle is in its ability to train and educate customers in a more effective and memorable way than text or static imagery.

Remember how the brain processes visual information and how we store it in long-term memory? The more effective the onboarding is, the faster your customer will learn your product or service, and the more proficient they will be in those critical first 30 days.

Using video can be particularly effective for customers who may not receive a dedicated one-on-one onboarding experience, giving you a way to scale your onboarding efficiently while still delivering an amazing experience.

While it may seem overwhelming at first to think about how you would transform your current onboarding experience into an on-demand library of visual content, the best approach is often to start small and simple. You don't need to "wow" customers with flashy content and clever scripts; onboarding videos can easily be recorded using webcams, screen capture software, and smartphones.

Keep it simple and direct, use your internal experts, and focus on clearly showing customers how to accomplish common tasks.

In many cases, shorter is better for onboarding videos!

Instead of creating a one-hour walkthrough of every feature and function, start by creating short "micro demos" for individual features, functions, or services. Each video could be less than five minutes long.

This approach gives you multiple advantages over creating longer form onboarding content.

First, it makes content creation simpler and more distributable. If you make a mistake while recording a short feature demo, you can simply start over without significant overhead. You can also tap different people across the marketing, sales and customer service teams to contribute different pieces of content.

Second, it makes your content easier to update as your products and services evolve. If instead, you record a one-hour video walking through your full product, and then a single feature changes, it may be frustrating and time-consuming to re-record the entire thing. But with the "micro-content" approach, you can simply re-record that short feature-specific video.

Finally, it makes your content more modular and customizable. For example, if a certain customer only has access to a limited set of features or services, you can create a customized playlist that walks through those specific features for a personalized viewing experience that aligns with what they have purchased.

When using video for customer onboarding, your primary goals are to help them be successful within their first 30 days and to ensure they have a positive brand experience as they roll out your solution.

With that in mind, start by focusing on the content that will have the biggest impact on achieving these short-term goals.

Chapter 56

HOW TO INCREASE ADOPTION AND EXPAND UTILIZATION

How many times have you purchased the most amazing product or service only to end up using a fraction of the capabilities that you were originally so excited about?

This is very common in today's business world, where customers purchase a product or service with aspirations to use all of the wonderful capabilities. In practice, however, they only end up adopting a small set of those features or services.

When this happens it can pose a serious risk for customer retention or repeat sales and can make trying to generate expansion or upsell opportunities next to impossible. Customer marketing can play a key role in helping to drive awareness, adoption, and utilization of key products and services—and video can be the perfect way to do it.

Imagine that you're nine months into an annual contract for your new internal finance system, *FinTastic.*

You purchased it with the goal of improving efficiencies across accounts payable, accounts receivable, and procurement. However, your deployment stalled after the first two groups due to shifting priorities, resource constraints, and lack of project ownership. If things continue in this fashion, your renewal call in three months is going to center around the fact that you aren't leveraging everything you paid for as opposed to what more you could be doing.

However, an email suddenly lands in your inbox with a short video called "FinTastic in 5 Minutes: Getting Started with Your Procurement Package." Could it be? Could it *really* be?

You click play and the delightful video features FinTastic's head of customer service showing you how to get started with a key feature you haven't yet activated. By the end of the video, you're not only ready to dive in and do it yourself, but you're thinking:

"Wow, their head of customer service is super nice, darn funny, and someone who I trust can help us get to the next level!"

Now, stop imagining this came from FinTastic and start thinking about this coming from *your* brand. Visual content gives you the opportunity to not only educate customers in a more effective way on products or services they may not be using to their full potential, it can also help to humanize your brand and showcase that you genuinely want to help them succeed.

The simple addition of a human face—a trusted authority on what you do—speaking in a casual and familiar tone can go a long way toward building rapport and humanizing your brand at scale.

Of course, this idea doesn't need to stop with product or service adoption. Video content can clearly demonstrate additional products and services that may lead to upsell and expansion opportunities.

Once a FinTastic customer has reached a certain level of maturity, why not send them another "FinTastic in 5 Minutes" video, but this time showcasing how they could *expand* their use into their accounting team to improve data accuracy?

When approaching this type of content, think creatively about how to make it fun, interesting, and a little bit more human. You're not trying to win them over as buyers; you're trying to connect with them as *real people* who have *real problems* you can help solve.

Chapter 57

HOW TO TURN CUSTOMERS INTO FANS THROUGH DELIGHTFUL DIGITAL EXPERIENCES

Customer marketing is now firing on all cylinders and you're seeing higher adoption, retention, and upsell metrics as a result. *Amazing!*

Now comes the fun stuff: turning your happy customers into raving fans. You know, the type of customer who would recommend you to others in an instant, would defend you publicly on social media and would leave a five-star review in a heartbeat.

This is something that most marketing teams don't consciously think about but, based on how buyer behaviors are changing, this can be an incredibly important part of any marketing and sales strategy. When you create raving fans, it not only helps you increase retention rates, it also transforms your current customer base into a source of new leads through authentic acts of advocacy, glowing online reviews, and word-of-mouth referrals.

There are a number of ways to use visual content to deliver truly delightful experiences that create these kinds of results.

HUMANIZING YOUR BRAND AND CREATE MORE PERSONAL CONNECTIONS

One of the easiest ways to delight customers is to use authentic video content to break down the digital divide between the people within your respective organizations.

The more familiar they are with the real people across your teams, the more connected they'll feel to your brand and the more likely they are to go to bat for you. If a customer has a dedicated account manager, chances are they've met them in person or via video conferencing.

But what about the scores of others across different teams who also contribute to their success?

The passionate execs, the dedicated developers, the heroic service reps, and even the amazing accountant who is trying to make their procurement process as seamless as possible.

There are numerous ways to get your people on camera to introduce themselves to new accounts. Much like creating "micro demos" for your products, you can also create "micro intros" for people across your company that can be used in different ways, as needed.

For example, when a new customer comes on board, send them a "Welcome to the Family" video that pulls in introductions from different people they may interact with over time. By the way, I'm not just talking about a formal introduction of name, title, and role. I'm talking about a personal, human introduction that has them laughing on camera, sharing their favorite recipe, showing off photos of their pets and kids—whatever it is that makes them tick as real people!

That's the kind of content that will truly delight a new customer and make them say:

"Wow, I'm genuinely excited to be working with these people!"

It's also the kind of content that gets shared around and builds your brand awareness "virally" within an account.

Once you create short videos that introduce your team members, they can be used in a variety of other ways. Each person can add their video intro as part of their standard email signature, giving anyone they interact with digitally the chance to get to know them. You can also use them on your website on your team page to humanize your brand and introduce your greatest assets to anyone researching your company.

Alternatively, you can create a fun series on your blog called "Meet the Team" and drip these videos out over time to allow your audience to get to know the real people who make all the magic happen.

What may seem like a simple idea can end up being an impactful and delightful experience for your customers and your broader community.

Chapter 58

HOW TO DELIGHT YOUR CUSTOMERS WITH WOW-WORTHY CULTURE-BASED VIDEO CONTENT

A second way to delight your customers is to deliver engaging and entertaining campaigns throughout the year that are purely designed to share your appreciation, showcase your culture and values, and build affinity towards your brand. It's the type of content that most marketing teams don't actively consider, but can be the most memorable and impactful to your existing customer base.

There's no one-size-fits-all solution for how each business can use culture videos to delight their customers. Generally speaking, inspiration needs to come from within and should be an authentic manifestation of your culture and values.

HOW WE DO THIS AT VIDYARD

At Vidyard, we take culture-based content seriously, as we've found time and again that the most meaningful responses we get from customers are when we strike an emotional chord and make them laugh, smile, or feel personally connected to the people on our team.

Some of our video content is planned out far in advance, whereas other videos are ad-hoc recordings based on trends, timely viral sensations, or industry news.

For example, when we see that a customer has made a major announcement (perhaps a funding raise, an acquisition, an IPO, a new CEO, etc.) we will bring the whole team together on camera to shout a mighty "CONGRATULATIONS!"

Typically, our CEO or head of customer experience champions this to make it even more impactful. We'll send that video directly to our champion and will also share it on social media. We consistently see heartfelt reactions from our customers to something that took less than five minutes to create and share.

A second example, our personalized holiday video, is my absolute favorite because of the heartfelt responses we've received from our customers, including:

"This is hands down one of my favorite emails ever." (Given the number of emails they likely receive, this one meant a lot!)

"OH EM GEEE. I love this and am sending it to everyone I know." (Yes, they even took the time to spell out the expanded version of OMG which is a clear signal you nailed it.)

"This might be the greatest gift I receive this year. You guys are awesome. Thank you!" (Our pleasure, truly.)

The day we got responses like these was the day we felt like we truly won as marketers.

Following that campaign, we not only experienced some of the highest engagement we've ever generated within our base, we also saw a significant impact on downstream pipeline and revenue from those who had watched the video.

In discussing this with our sales team, we learned that this video acted as a trigger for many of our customers to reach back out to their account manager to thank them for the delightful experience, which in many cases turned into a casual conversation about how we could help them further in the following year.

 To watch the video for yourself, check out **www.thevisualsale.com**, and keep in mind that each customer received a unique version of the video that was personalized for them, adding significantly to the delight factor.

Some other examples of how to use culture videos to turn customers into fans include:

- **Videos to celebrate customer lifecycle milestones,** such as a "happy anniversary" video to celebrate their yearly anniversary of being a customer. There are lots of ways to have fun with this one and put a smile on their face!
- **Videos of your team members participating in timely trends** or internet challenges. Our own Mannequin Challenge video from back in 2016 is one of our most-watched videos of all time, with

many customers commenting on how much they loved it. And it took less than 20 minutes to record and edit.

- **Videos sharing stories from any giveback or corporate social responsibility** (CSR) programs your company may invest in, or other programs that showcase the culture and passion of your people.

- **Fun and creative videos at the end or beginning of the calendar year** to thank your customers for another great year and to get them excited about what is to come.

- **Lighthearted videos to celebrate other holidays and culture days** throughout the year such as Halloween, April Fool's Day, or Valentine's Day. Every February, our marketing team turns a meeting room into a Valentine's Day 'video booth' that our sales reps use to record personal video messages to remind their customers how much they care.

Delightful content like this can go a long way in humanizing your brand and making your customers feel more connected to your business and your people. And that feeling will go a long way in making them brand advocates and possibly even raving fans!

As an added benefit, your own employees may actually find the experience of creating content like this, and hearing the responses from your customers, just as delightful.

Chapter 59

AXONIFY TRANSFORMS CUSTOMER ENGAGEMENT WITH VIDEO

Have you ever subscribed to a vendor's newsletter or followed them on social media not because you're interested in what they do, but because you *love* their marketing and want to follow them for inspiration? *Me, too.*

Now, have you ever bought a product from a company just to get on their customer marketing list? *Me neither.* But if I were to do that, I'd buy myself a license to Axonify's platform to be inspired by their amazing customer marketing and communications.

Axonify is a rapidly growing software-as-a-service (SaaS) provider in the employee training and learning space. Their platform helps businesses transform the way they approach employee training by offering customized learning paths for each individual employee to fill knowledge gaps in a personalized way.

In many respects, Axonify has two very different user profiles within each of their accounts they need to keep engaged and make successful: the individual(s) administering the overall employee training program (typically, HR professionals) and the employees within that business who are the end consumers of the training programs. If either the administrators or end users don't see value in the platform, they can quickly become a churn risk.

On the flip side, if product adoption is strong and brand sentiment is high, there may be a significant opportunity for expansion, upsells, and referrals. As a result, Carrie Cardoso Côté sees her role as much more than just customer communications.

> *"The customers who use more features of the platform and see higher employee engagement are the ones most likely to renew their contract and expand their deployment. Our account management team is responsible for ensuring individual clients are successful, particularly those with larger deployments, and they do a fantastic job.*
>
> *But our customer marketing team plays a key role in delivering one-to-many programs across all of our customer tiers to generate awareness and adoption of new product features, to educate administrators on how to increase utilization by their employees, and to delight them with experiences that humanize our business and increase brand affinity.*
>
> *The result is higher renewal rates, improved net promoter score (NPS), new expansion and upsell opportunities, on a closer connection to our brand and our people."*
>
> **Carrie Cardoso Côté, Head of Customer Marketing at Axonify**

While Axonify invests in a number of different programs to communicate with their customers throughout the year, video has emerged as an incredibly powerful way to engage, educate, and delight their users.

Through a combination of agency-produced, in-house created, and do-it-yourself webcam, and screen capture videos, the customer marketing and account management teams now use video to support virtually every aspect of the post-sale customer experience. And it all begins as soon as they sign the contract.

HOW AXONIFY EMBRACED VIDEO AT EVERY STAGE OF THE CUSTOMER LIFECYCLE

One of the most important stages of the customer lifecycle is initial onboarding and training. While their account management team provides customized onboarding for many new clients, this approach wasn't able to scale as Axonify's lower-tier customer base expanded and as new administrators took over the helm within existing accounts.

To create a more scalable onboarding solution, while preserving the feel of "white glove" service, they invested in a series of onboarding, training, and how-to videos to enable new users to quickly ramp up via on-demand content. More than just a set of tutorials, the videos offer clear and concise walk-throughs of how to accomplish common tasks to ensure those who are new to the platform can get up to speed with nothing being lost in translation.

Once the customer is successfully launched and starting to see value from the solution, the role of customer marketing shifts to driving feature adoption and keeping users engaged in the platform—*this is when the real magic happens.*

Automated email nurturing sequences now start to drip through to each customer with tailored content to help guide them on their journey as an Axonify customer.

Short explainer videos expose them to new features that haven't yet been activated, showing them exactly how they work and the benefits they offer. A branded video series called **Meet the Features** is introduced as a fun way to learn about other aspects of the platform. Shot in the style of a television dating show, each feature is personified by an individual on their account team where they vie for your attention and hope to be the next feature that you turn on and take out for a date.

The entertainment factor makes the content highly approachable, easy to consume, and (dare I say) *binge-worthy*. The result? Their customer walks away more educated and more likely to discover a new feature that they need to start using, which may result in an upgrade!

In addition to incorporating videos into their automated nurture streams, Axonify turned their new product release notes into video-based content with massive success.

Prior to this initiative, new product releases were supported with text-based emails and knowledge articles summarizing the updates, fixes, and new features available. However, the click-through rate and engagement in that content was low, resulting in missed opportunities for new product adoption.

That all changed with video.

Each product release is now supported with a short video clearly explaining what's new and what the related benefits are. With video, they can show exactly how it works, while building a greater sense of connection by featuring their own employees, executives, and even product developers.

This simple move from text-based to video-based release notes has helped Axonify significantly increase customer engagement and new feature adoption.

IT GETS EVEN MORE DELIGHTFUL

My favorite part of this story is how Axonify then uses creative video concepts to truly *delight* their customers and to build an ongoing brand relationship. For example, during each of the last three years, Axonify has put in some extra effort to wish their customers a "happy holiday" in a way that shows they truly care.

During the month of December, while most businesses are busy sending out disposable greeting cards and templated holiday emails, Axonify truly delights each customer with a highly anticipated personalized holiday video that tells a fun and memorable story.

Playing off of well known holiday stories such *The Polar Express* and *How the Grinch Stole Christmas*—and using Vidyard's automated video personalization technology to literally bring each viewer into the story—Axonify's creative storytelling bestows true holiday cheer and generates responses like:

"Absolutely fabulous . . . est card I have ever received. Please share my feedback with the whole Axonify Team. It's been a great year, looking forward to more great things next year."

"OK, that's pretty fantastic! Great job, looking forward to sharing with my team. You'll be hearing a lot from me in 2018 when I will be focusing more on taking our online training to the next level!"

To receive feedback like that as a B2B brand is truly exceptional and rewarding. But does it really matter? Does it actually help with long-term results?

Ask one of their customers, a large telecommunications company, who had been unresponsive for months despite efforts from Axonify's customer marketing and account management teams to get their attention. They responded to this video email almost immediately and *then* expanded their deployment after re-engaging in conversations following the holiday.

Axonify has used equally creative videos to boost engagement in their quarterly customer campaigns, drive awareness of their annual customer event, and increase registrations in their loyalty program. They even humanized their executives through a parody of James Corden's viral *Carpool Karaoke!* Because, well, is there any better way to create an emotional bond with your customers than to have them watch slightly embarrassing videos of your execs singing karaoke with other customers?

Nope, there's simply *no* better way.

> *"We went from having little one-to-many communication with our customers outside of release notes, to building a full-fledged calendar of automated communications where video plays an integral role at every stage. Customers now expect—and love—the educational and entertaining videos we share regularly to help them be better with Axonify.*
>
> *Customers are watching 100% of our videos, even for those that span close to four minutes! Feedback is overwhelmingly positive from our customers, as well as our own internal employees, who truly appreciate how we've used video to share our knowledge in a more effective way and to connect on a more personal and human level."*
>
> **Carrie Cardoso Côté, Head of Customer Marketing at Axonify**

Chapter 60

VIDEO FOR CUSTOMER MARKETING CHECKLIST

When it comes to building more personal relationships with your customers at scale, video is the next best thing to being there in person.

The following checklist outlines best practices on how to use video in your customer marketing program to drive product or service adoption, increase retention rates, and turn everyday customers into raving advocates:

☐ **Use video-based tutorials to deliver exceptional onboarding and training at scale**
Self-service content can be the most effective and efficient way for new customers to learn how to implement, deploy, or customize their new product or service. Use on-demand videos to educate your customers in a way that is clear, easy to follow, *and* builds your brand along the way!

☐ **Use targeted video content to drive adoption and utilization**Create short and engaging videos that clearly explain the benefits of key features or products, and show exactly how to start using them. Publish these videos in a customer knowledge center, include them in your customer newsletter, and add them to ongoing customer communications to maximize awareness and adoption of key capabilities.

☐ **Use video to humanize your brand and connect your customers to your people**
Create a more personal and emotional connection to your brand as a way of increasing retention and upsell/cross-sell rates. Use creative videos featuring your own employees in ongoing customer communications, updates, promotions, and to showcase your giveback programs. Use video to establish empathy and a more personal connection with the real people within your business.

☐ **Delight your customers and stay top-of-mind with culture-based content**
Use culture-based videos to let your guard down and have some fun! Create fun, engaging, and even personalized videos to celebrate the holidays, get in on a pop culture trend, or to congratulate your customers on a major milestone. Take your relationship from B2B or B2C to H2H—human-to-human!

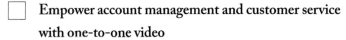

☐ **Empower account management and customer service with one-to-one video**

Take your visual customer engagement strategy from one-to-many to one-to-one by empowering your account management team with the tools they need to deliver video-based messaging and communications. Refer to the next section of this book for all the information you need on how to deliver a visual account management experience.

Chapter 61

HOW TO PRIORITIZE YOUR VIDEO MARKETING EFFORTS

So many ideas! But where do I start?

I'll be the first to admit that there was a lot to digest in this section on video in marketing. My co-workers have never accused me of being light on details or short on ideas!

But at the risk of overwhelming you, I wanted to share a broad range of examples and best practices since no two businesses are alike.

Can you go off and implement all of these ideas next week? No.

Is every use-case we discussed a priority for *your* business? Likely not.

So, how should you prioritize *your* video marketing efforts?

Like most things in marketing and sales, start with the content that will have the most immediate impact on customers and revenue.

Identify where you have challenges or inefficiencies in your current buyer's journey and use video to address those head on!

If your greatest challenge is building an audience, start with educational videos for inbound marketing, social media, YouTube, and your blog. Focus on generating awareness and building your brand through helpful and human video content.

If you have a strong online audience, but your website performance is lagging, focus on using video strategically on your website, landing pages, and pricing page to reduce your bounce rate and increase conversions.

If you have a strong database of leads but are struggling to convert them into sales opportunities, look for ways to use video in your content marketing, email marketing, and outbound demand generation programs to earn their attention and show them exactly what they're missing out on.

And if you're part of a larger business with dedicated marketing teams for different programs and channels, share the appropriate chapter of this book with each team to start tackling these ideas in parallel. Every team can benefit from using video!

But as you start to implement these ideas on your path to becoming a video-enabled business, there is one critical factor that can make or break your long-term success.

You must create a culture of video and embrace in-house video creation.

Not just within marketing, but across your entire business, and it starts at the top.

PART VII

CREATING THE CULTURE OF VIDEO... IN-HOUSE

Chapter 62

WHY YOUR BUSINESS NEEDS AN IN-HOUSE VIDEOGRAPHER

So, let's assume you feel video—and "showing it"—is fundamental to your business going forward. You've bought into the idea that it starts with sales, you see the tremendous opportunities we've discussed with marketing, and now you want to bring it all together.

If you do want to become a "media company" and produce great, impactful content, how are you going to do it?

In order for this to happen, you must embrace two important realities:

- Someone must "own" (at least eventually) your video production in-house—i.e. a videographer.

- Your team must clearly understand the what, how, and why of video, while also being willing to learn how to effectively communicate on camera.

Your immediate reaction upon reading this is very likely the same thought so many business owners and managers have told me over the past few years as I've spoken on this subject:

"Why would a business like mine ever have the need for a full-time videographer? And is there really 40 hours of work per week for such a position in my niche?"

To answer the first question, let's just go back to all the types of sales and marketing videos Tyler and I have written about up to this point. These videos, when done well, are likely going to take a videographer months and months to produce.

Let's look at it another way.

My agency, IMPACT, has worked hand-in-hand with organizations across a wide range of industries with video, and never have we seen a situation where we said, "You know, there simply isn't enough work here for a videographer to work full-time."

Besides that, if you truly understand where this is all headed and the incredible importance the videographer position will have on your sales and marketing numbers, you would never blink as to whether or not this should be a full-time position.

With all the successful customers we've worked with, we've never, after the first year of doing video, had anyone question the need for this position. Rather, most are debating, "Should we hire another?"

The last argument I'll make for the videographer before discussing what to look for in this person is this:

In 10 years, the position of "videographer" will be just as important and prominent to an organization's success as a "sales manager" is today.

You might be thinking to yourself, "No way. You're crazy."

But it's true.

Today, most organizations see the position of "sales manager" as critical and important to their success. The same will be true for videographers in the very near future—as their financial impact from a sales perspective, will often be more significant than that of the sales manager's.

OK, now that we've discussed the need to hire a videographer, let's look at exactly "how" you can find the perfect person to lead the video production efforts for your organization going forward.

Because this position can and will have such a massive impact on your success, it's not something you'll want to rush or take lightly. Doing it right the first time will be well worth it in the long run.

At IMPACT, we have assisted hundreds of clients and organizations in their search for a videographer. As you might imagine, we've made some great hires and also seen our share of complete duds.

Zach Basner, IMPACT's director of inbound training and video strategy, has led our efforts in growing the educational video department of the agency and has found the following to be essential steps in this process.

Chapter 63

IDENTIFYING THE PERSONALITY TRAITS OF A VIDEOGRAPHER

As the videographer, the person who fills this position will be the visual storyteller of the company.

As such, they need to be a great fit within the culture of your business. They will have frequent contact with employees within the organization and, in certain scenarios, will have to give and receive criticism to develop the best content. Somebody who is uncomfortable, overly introverted, or doesn't mesh well with the company culture you've established won't succeed in this role.

It's also important to look for a strong desire for personal growth within your videographer candidates.

Each video they create will hopefully be better than the last, so you really want your videographer to take feedback well. Also, because video technology is evolving at such a rapid rate, this desire for personal development and continual learning is absolutely essential.

Also, consider this—the videographer is probably going to be the only employee (or one of a select few) who focuses on video, so they can't rely on a manager or colleague to help them when it comes to the technicalities of video production.

During the interview process, focus heavily on seeking out the following traits in your videographer hire:

- They are able to work with a team or on their own.
- They own the production process and do what it takes to make great content.
- They are self-starting and treat the brand as if it were their own.
- They deal well with constructive criticism and are able to receive feedback easily.
- They have great communication skills and are able to interview and make people comfortable.
- They are energetic and able to excite others on the team to be on camera.
- They look at the content from the eye of the viewer to create the best experience.
- They are lifelong learners and eager to identify new learning opportunities.

More often than not, assuming they have the video production skills, someone who is fun and energetic is going to be a great candidate for this role.

Because many people within your organization might not particularly enjoy being in front of a camera (especially at first), their ability to inspire others is arguably as important as their ability to use the camera.

Chapter 64

THE IDEAL VIDEOGRAPHER BACKGROUND

A common question businesses ask is, "Should our candidate have earned a degree in video production or something comparable?"

Although having a degree is generally a great sign, don't see it as a moral imperative. Especially with the proliferation of video production within today's younger generation, it's not unusual to see phenomenal content that had almost no "formal" training behind it.

Remember, this is a "creative" position. Ultimately, their practical skills will make all the difference.

Here is a quick list our company uses that should guide you in the proper direction when making a hire:

POTENTIAL FIELDS OF STUDY

- Journalism
- Education
- Video production
- Graphic design
- Photography

TECHNICAL SKILLS

- Proficient with video editing software (Adobe Premiere or Final Cut Pro are the most common)
- Experience with Adobe After Effects or Motion is preferred
- Experience with Adobe Photoshop and Adobe Illustrator is a plus
- Can conduct research and purchase needed equipment
- Can operate and maintain proper levels and calibration of cameras, audio and video recorders, and other production equipment
- Embraces new technology, such as augmented reality (AR), virtual reality (VR), etc., as it happens
- Understands the importance of tracking video marketing metrics

CREATIVE SKILLS

- Proficient at storyboarding, scripting, and concepting
- Understands basic and advanced composition techniques
- Understands the fundamentals of branding
- Detail-oriented and able to identify quality issues in audio and video others might miss

- Understands the basics of social media platforms, native social video, and content promotion through social channels

VIDEO PORTFOLIO

- Has a YouTube, Instagram, or Vimeo channel
- Has a personal website with a portfolio

These are just some ideas of how to gauge experience and skill level. However, know that not all videographer candidates are going to meet all of the criteria we've mentioned above.

There is one important thing you need to remember—your candidate must display traits that lend themselves to business storytelling and not just cinematic knowledge.

Granted, this can be trained and taught, but don't lose sight of the fact that, just because someone is good at "making videos," doesn't mean they are skilled at the art of producing sales and marketing videos.

Chapter 65

INTERVIEW QUESTIONS FOR VIDEOGRAPHER CANDIDATES

If your candidate has already passed the company culture fit screening, has the technical and creative skills required, and is equipped with a stellar video portfolio, you're on track.

Here are a few more interview questions you can ask your candidates during the interview and throughout the rest of the hiring process that will yield valuable insights into a candidate's capabilities as a videographer, as well as how successful they'll be at your company:

- What's your favorite part of video editing? What is your least favorite?

- What websites or resources do you use to learn new strategies and techniques, and improve your skills?

- What don't you like about the video production process?
- What are the most important steps in pre-production?
- Tell me about a time when your footage didn't turn out as you had hoped. What did you learn? How did you fix it?
- Who are some of your favorite videographers, channels, or influencers? (If they don't have any, this could be a sign they don't love learning.)
- What makes a perfect visual story?
- What videos have you seen online that were poorly done?
- When you see someone doing something wrong on camera, how do you generally offer feedback? Can you provide specific examples of those instances?
- How, specifically, do you deal with someone who doesn't feel comfortable on camera?
- What's the toughest piece of feedback or criticism you've ever received for some of your work? Was it valid? (Self-awareness is essential for this position.)
- In your opinion, what makes a business video different from, say, a short film?
- From what you know about our company so far, what's an important element of telling our story that's missing?
- What do you feel are the most important videos our company could produce right now?

As you can see by these questions, it's important that you find out how knowledgeable they are, how well they receive feedback, and if they're up for the challenge of making amazing videos for your organization.

Then, once you've vetted your candidates with these specific interview questions, it's time for the practical challenge.

Chapter 66

A SIMPLE VIDEO ASSIGNMENT AS PART OF THE INTERVIEW PROCESS

What videographer interview process would be complete without seeing what the candidate is capable of?

That's where the practical video assignment comes in.

By this point, your candidate has probably "talked the talk" during the interview process but now let's see if they can "walk the walk" by actually creating a video to your specifications.

This assignment not only shows you the candidate's video skills, it will also tell you a lot about their time management, creativity, critical thinking, and communication skills.

Here's what you should ask them to do:

- **Have your videographer candidates make a video explaining why they want the job.** This will give you an idea of how effective they are at telling a story. Also, how they present themselves could give you an idea of how well they understand your brand.

- **Give a specific timeframe to complete the video—between two and five days.** This shows how well they perform under a time constraint, how fast they are able to turnaround content, and how creative they can be under pressure.

- **Have them develop a script or storyboard to accompany the video.** This shows their creative process beyond the cameras and lights. Many times this is what they'll be presenting when they start a new project. How prepared can they be?

- **Allow them to be creative, and think outside the scope of a traditional marketing video.** Let them know that they are free to tell the story as they wish to tell it, so be creative and have fun with it.

So, there you have it. When hiring a videographer for your company, don't skip any of the steps we've outlined. And please, don't see your organization as the exception.

We know that we must show it, and not just say it.

A full-time videographer working hand-in-hand with the rest of your team can very well make this possible.

*To get a sample videographer job description, just go to **thevisualsale.com**.*

Chapter 67

TEAM BUY-IN ON VIDEO, PERFORMANCE TIPS, AND LONG-TERM SUCCESS

Now that we've established our goal to become a media company, are embracing all the types of videos you've read herein, and have found the right videographer—we still have one major obstacle in front of us:

GETTING YOUR TEAM ENGAGED AND BOUGHT-IN WITH VIDEO.

Just as we discussed earlier in this book, so much of digital sales and marketing success with any business starts with a basic understanding of the what, how, and why of video. Only then can it become a culture of who you are, thus allowing you to achieve your greatest potential.

Over the past few years, I've been shocked at how many companies have approached me and said:

"Marcus, we tried video. But after we hired a video production company and attempted to produce these videos, we realized something—we're just not good on camera."

Alas, the "we're just not good on camera" mindset strikes again.

I've traveled the globe speaking to audiences about sales and marketing and this literally may be the No. 1 excuse made by audience members when pushing back on video—well, other than the claim of, "but my business is different."

But think of it this way— what would members of your sales team say if you asked them, "Are you good with people?"

If they are like 99% of the sales professionals I've spoken to, they'd immediately pipe up and say, "Oh yes, I'm very good with people."

Think about that for a second.

Why is it that most of us would say we're good with people yet terrible on camera?

It's simply not the case, which is why the moment you and your team start seeing the camera as a person—yes, I really mean that—and not as a camera, everything starts to change. I have personally witnessed this again and again.

Over the past few years, I've spent hours training sales teams and other subject matter experts on how to be effective on camera.

With a few tips and techniques—and a little practice—it truly is remarkable how quickly one can get not just comfortable, but also effective, on camera.

While we can't present an exhaustive analysis of on-camera performance in this book, I want to give you enough to get started with your team, which is why we'll discuss the three most fundamental rules of on-camera success.

If you commit to following these three rules and make them a part of your company culture, you'll be amazed at how quickly your team starts to perform and communicate effectively on camera.

RULE NO. 1: DON'T STOP

Have you ever watched a live TV weather reporter "just keep going" in the middle of a hurricane or storm? Ever wondered how they do it?

Well, for the most part, they have one simple rule:

You can't stop, no matter what.

This is what makes live TV special.

The same holds true when you shoot video with your team. Your people need to understand that, regardless of what they say or how they say it, to simply "keep going"—no matter what.

This is true due to three realities:

- The moment someone knows they can stop while being recorded is the moment they will start stopping a lot more.

- Most mistakes we make on camera can be fixed by a videographer in post-production.

- By moving forward and finishing, you "work out the kinks" in what you're attempting to say—almost like writing the first draft to an article—therefore allowing it to be said better the second time.

If you think about the "don't stop" rule, it's actually something your sales team has followed for years.

For example, when was the last time one of them was on a sales call with a prospect or customer and suddenly said, "Oops, I messed up what

I was trying to say. Let's just start the whole conversation over again, shall we?"

Yep, sales professionals learn early on that they must keep going, regardless of what happens or what is said in the moment. This exact same mindset should be applied to video communication as well.

RULE NO. 2: BUT YOU CAN DO IT AGAIN

Although we don't want to stop in the middle of a take or segment, it is absolutely fine to do it again once completed.

Often, because we're "working it out"—figuring out what we're trying to say—with the first take, the way we deliver the message may not be as fluid or incisive as we would like it to be.

It's surprising just how well we will say it the second try—bigger smile, more concise, greater clarity—assuming we continue to follow the "don't stop" rule.

This being said, if you and your team are following these rules but still need more than three or four attempts to "say it right," then there is a good chance you should move on to another video—especially one you're more comfortable and familiar with.

RULE NO. 3: THE 3-SECOND SMILE

A wise man once said, "By small and simple things are great things brought to pass."

The same is true with video communication—particularly when it comes to the magic of the smile.

Yes, the smile.

"OK, Marcus. I already know it's important to smile."

I know you know this, but the reality is most people forget this simple truth the moment the camera's red recording light comes on.

The specific technique we teach at IMPACT is so utterly simple, you may be tempted to disregard it. But don't, because it works.

Here it is:

Start smiling three seconds before hitting the record button.

Yes, three seconds.

Why?

The first reason is because, once the video starts, you want to be coming off of your smile, not going into it. This establishes an immediate tone that is warm, friendly, and trustworthy. The second reason goes back to the subject of nerves. It's much harder to be nervous when you're truly smiling than when you're not. If you don't believe me, try. It works.

Therefore, make this a major habit with your team. Practice the three-second smile rule with every video and the results will follow.

Chapter 68

THE PROBLEM
WITH SCRIPTS

One of the questions I'm asked most by companies attempting to ingratiate video in their culture is whether or not they should be using scripts.

To answer this question, think of it this way:

When was the last time one of your sales team members was in a sales appointment and, after being asked a question by a prospect said, "Hmm, good question, let me pull out my script and read you the answer"?

Again, it very likely has never happened.

So, if sales professionals don't use scripts when they're face-to-face with prospects or customers, why would they use them on videos?

Plus, the moment you (as a viewer) watch a video and realize someone is reading from a script is the moment you start to lose trust in that person and doubt their subject matter expertise.

Each person on your team is an expert in some way, shape, or form. They are used to answering questions. In fact, many have answered thousands over the years. So, allow them to talk to the camera exactly like they would with a prospect.

Does this mean you don't have some type of potential order or even a rudimentary outline sketched out for the video? No, it does not.

As Tyler mentioned earlier, preparation absolutely matters. But focus more on being as real and human as possible, rather than saying it in such a rote and robotic manner.

Chapter 69

GETTING BUY-IN AND EMBRACING THE MESSY

Again, do not make the mistake of bringing in a video production company and just "throwing" your team on camera. This strategy, without question, will almost always do more harm than good.

Just like with everything else we've discussed, your people must understand the what, how, and why of video. They need on-camera performance training.

Does this take much time?

No, definitely not.

In all frankness, everything we've discussed here on video can be covered in one day with your team. My agency has taught well over 100 workshops and trainings on video and they do not need to be nearly as complex as some people believe.

What does take time, though, is the simple willingness to "embrace the messy" that comes with creating a culture of video. Like anything else that really matters in business, there is a learning curve here.

Just as Tyler mentioned at the beginning of this book, it's going to be clunky.

Not all videos will come out as you hoped.

Not everyone is going to be great on camera the first day.

Not every video will take off as anticipated.

But it will be worth it.

So, embrace the messy. Get through the learning curve, and when you come out on the other side, you'll ultimately humanize and add soul to your business in a way you never realized would be possible.

Having worked with so many companies on this, I know this is true. You, too, will experience this for yourself.

Chapter 70

VIRTUAL SELLING, THE FUTURE OF SALES IN THE DIGITAL AGE

For years, I've been asking my sales team at River Pools and Spas the same question:

*"Why can't we sell **virtually**?"*

In other words, why can't we use a basic video conferencing tool (e.g., ZOOM) to meet with our prospects, instead of always making the long drive to their home for a sales call?

But old habits die hard, and no one on the team took the initiative to make the change.

After all, the old adage of "nose-to-nose, face-to-face" — which underscores the critical importance of in-person interactions — is something many sales professionals live and die by.

That is until the novel coronavirus (COVID-19) pandemic of 2020, of course.

Seemingly overnight, thousands of businesses around the world retreated into their homes to work remotely full-time due to new government-imposed public health restrictions. As a result, suddenly "nose-to-nose, face-to-face" (at least as we'd always known it) was longer a viable approach for sales teams.

At River Pools specifically, the pain of "social distancing" pushed us to do something that we should have been doing years beforehand. But we avoided it until this "new normal" forced our hand:

We had to sell our in-ground swimming pools to customers virtually.

Knowing we had to act quickly, in mid-March of 2020, just as COVID-19 was beginning to have seemingly devastating consequences for the United States economy, we made one simple change to the "request a quote" page of our company website.

We added the following question to our forms:

"Would you like a virtual sales experience?"

It seems like a very small adjustment, right? Well, overnight, the leads started pouring in, with 90% of those filling out the form saying, "Yes, I would love to have a virtual sales appointment."

To further enhance this new sales approach, we also produced a "how-to" video for potential customers showing them how to take photos of their property, therefore allowing our sales team and designers to "see" the backyard.

With those photos, our team could then provide an accurate quote for a new in-ground swimming pool to a motivated potential buyer without having to physically *be* in the backyard.

Within weeks of adopting this new methodology, every sales team member was, quite literally smitten.

In fact, one of our reps recently said, "I've been selling pools for years, and this has forced me to realize I've been wasting a whole lot of time. I'm never going back to the way I was doing it before."

Now, instead of spending up to three hours driving to and from an in-person sales appointment — which alone also lasted about two hours — sales reps only had to dedicate a single hour to a sales appointment. And they could do so within the comfort of their own home.

As you can imagine, the efficiency, on both a personal and professional level, quickly went through the roof. Our sales team members could now complete three entire sales appointments one evening… and still have time to sit down and eat dinner with their family.

Looking ahead, regardless of what a post-coronavirus "normal" looks like, there is no question in my mind. Our sales team will not be going back to the old ways of selling. Virtual selling will be an instrumental part of our future sales success strategy.

A stunning development considering they pushed back on this for so long, wouldn't you say?

The lesson here is that change, even when positive, is disruptive by its very nature. In fact, change of any kind is hard. That is until you are presented, particularly as a business, with a "do or die" scenario.

Then it gets really easy.

In the case of River Pools, our sales team went from being essentially unemployed to having their best sales numbers ever — all because of this newfound virtual sales process we were forced to embrace with open arms and without hesitation.

Fascinating, indeed.

But, as you're well aware, River Pools and Spas isn't unique in this trend.

Sales as we know it for every business — whether you're B2B or B2C — is going to become more and more virtual going forward.

Before COVID-19, "nose-to-nose, face-to-face" only encompassed those moments where you were standing in front of someone, in-person. Now, it will include virtual meetings, where video conferencing technology will be the bridge that brings you together.

This being said, there are certain complexities that come with virtual selling — especially when it comes to video conferencing on a platform like ZOOM or GoToMeeting.

My digital sales and marketing company, IMPACT, has been conducting virtual sales calls via Zoom for three years. And now, after having trained so many sales teams on what an effective virtual selling approach looks like — and watching their common mistakes — I've found there are clear and universal virtual selling "best practices" with video conferencing.

Although they may come across as simple or obvious, I can assure you that they are often overlooked, especially when teams are first adjusting to this new way of selling.

11 IRREFUTABLE LAWS OF EFFECTIVE VIRTUAL SALES MEETINGS

1. Never assume your prospect or customer understands the technology (ZOOM, GoToMeeting, etc.) and has been on it before

You know what they say about "assuming" anything, right? So, while you may think your prospect or customer has a clear understanding of how your video conferencing platform works, they may not. Therefore, you should find this information out before your meeting, and send along a quick explainer video that reviews the basics of whichever platform you're using.

Of course, COVID-19 has forced people all over the world, young and old, to learn how to use video conferencing tools. And with most family practice doctor offices now even offering virtual doctor appointments, the overall familiarity everywhere has gone to levels we never previously imagined possible in such a short period of time.

2. You must require that cameras be on for all parties, no exceptions

Studies have shown that closing rates are more than 10% higher when the prospect has their camera on, which makes total sense. I mean, think about it — when you've done a video conference call and the other party didn't turn on their camera, how did the meeting go? Could you even tell if they were truly focused on what you were saying?

While it may feel uncomfortable at first, you must not be passive about this requirement. So, when preparing the prospect for the meeting, say something like:

3. Use less text in any presentation slides you prepare

If your slide-deck is a full-blown brochure, then send it to them before or after the sales appointment. But *never* makes the slides the hero nor centerpiece of a virtual sales call. Ever. When you rely on text-heavy slide presentations, your prospect or customer will spend much less time listening to the words coming out of your mouth, because their brain is occupied reading the words you've put in front of them. It's a competition you'll never win.

4. If you are using a slide deck, turn "sharing" mode on and off throughout the presentation, so as to induce better conversation

The more the prospect sees of you, and the more you see of them, the better. So if you're sharing a slide deck or image on your screen and know you're getting ready to launch into a discussion where the deck doesn't need to be shown, do everyone a favor and *stop sharing*.

By following this simple best practice, the prospect will now see more of you — as your video screen will be larger — and you'll see more of them. There will be less distraction by not showing anything else on your screen.

5. If you are meeting with a group of people — and they're sitting around a table or in a boardroom — write everyone's name down first

Ever forgotten someone's name during a sales call? Yeah, that's not good. *At all.* And because many virtual sales meetings consist of one group of people sitting in a boardroom or office together, the clear best practice is to ask everyone their name at the very beginning of the conversation, write each down in your notes, and then proceed to #6.

If you're worried about remaining whose name is whose, forgo a simple list and make a quick sketch of the table on a piece of paper. Then write down the names where each person is seated around that table.

6. When meeting with a group, always ask questions directly to the various attendees by *name*

By using this technique of referencing someone's name whenever you ask a question, you get everyone engaged and involved in the conversation. Remember, in virtual sales calls, you're almost always better off calling on a single person than you are asking an open question for the group — something most sales people consistently get wrong.

When you ask questions openly to a group, you will often unintentionally create awkward moments in the conversation because attendees may be too shy or timid to speak up, for fear of talking over someone else. By singling an individual out every time you ask a question, you'll greatly improve the flow of the conversation and earn more trust with the entire audience because of their mutual engagement.

7. Smile — a lot

We all think we smile and look happy in sales meetings... until we watch our first video sales call recording and realize we've got one heck of a "resting B-face." Even when you're not in a good mood, I'm sure you've noticed that having a genuine, warm smile on your face positively impacts our disposition and how we come across to others. So, although this recommendation may seem trite or insignificant, failing to smile or present in a friendly approachable manner is a major weakness of many sales professionals.

The other reason why smiling is so important is that when you meet with a prospect in real life, they are able to see all of you, from head to toe. In a video conversation though, they will likely only see you from the chest upward. This means the more you smile and project a positive disposition, the greater impact you'll have on the mood and energy of the call.

8. Face the light

Ever had a video call with someone that had a massive window behind them with the light shining in, blurring them out and causing you as the viewer to squint in the process? Yep, we've all been there. This is exactly why it's so important to face the light (have it in front of you) instead of having it located behind you.

In fact, you're better off in most cases to have one frontal light or window (facing you) and no lights on at all behind you. Another simple trick is to turn the brightness on your computer monitor all the way up.

9. Sit Straight Up or Stand

Your best communication will rarely occur sitting back, slouched in a chair. This is why, even though most sales folks don't think it matters, the majority of speakers and communicators perform at a significantly higher level when they're standing up than when they're sitting down.

As the saying goes in the speaking world, *"You'll never get a standing ovation by sitting down."*

So, invest in a stand-up desk for sales calls — or, heck, stack a bunch of books and boxes up on a table — and watch the difference it makes on camera… and your close rates.

10. Be definitive in the purpose of the call from the very beginning.

Like many of the best practices on this list, this may sound obvious, but it's even more important with video. Why? Well, in most cases, your prospects and buyers will not be aware of "where" the meeting is supposed to go — likely because they will have never done a virtual sales appointment before, for your particular product or service.

Therefore, tell them the purpose. Make it clear what you're going to cover, what defines success within the context of your discussion, and anything else that will help everyone on the call see exactly where the meeting is supposed to be headed.

11. Take control of the meeting — *please!*

It's your meeting. Own it.

If something is a distraction, call it out and fix it.. If someone needs to be muted, mute them. If your discussion needs to get back on track, guide it back swiftly. Do everything with tact, of course. But remember, the momentary discomfort will be well worth it in the end once you've gained the customer's trust and, ultimately, earned their business.

As mentioned earlier, although each of these may seem like "minor" suggestions, added up they will make a major difference in your team's sales success.

Additionally, keep in mind that one other major benefit of using video conferencing tools for sales is the fact that you can so easily record the call.

Doing this allows for a dramatically improved and effective training program with your team — one where you can "look at game tape" and offer coaching and advice on where your team (or you, for that matter) can do better.

WHAT'S AHEAD

As we look ahead at this evolution of video conferencing for sales, please keep this absolutely critical reality in mind:

Anything that you and I think *must* be sold face-to-face will eventually be sold digitally and online.

There are no exceptions to this reality, no matter how "different" you think your product, service, or industry might be.

I do not make this statement with a smile. I also don't have an agenda — it's a reality I've had to adjust to myself, as a business owner. It simply is what it is. It's what the marketplace (you, me, all of us) is asking for.

And because of this trend, we must start re-thinking the way we sell.

We must redefine things like "regional sales rep."

We must start offering a virtual sales option to our prospects and customers immediately.

If we don't, we run the inevitable risk of being left behind.

So, embrace this "new normal." Will it be messy converting to a virtual selling process? Yes, it sure will. In time, however, your team will get it, as with any change.

More importantly, your customers are going to be grateful for it. And, ultimately, your business will be dramatically better because of it.

Chapter 71

"BUT I'M JUST NOT GOOD ON CAMERA"

Before we end our journey together, there is one last story I want to share with you that represents everything "embrace the messy" represents.

I was once hired by a large real estate firm to train their agents on how to better communicate on camera.

To do the training, we brought my video team to a high-end property they were attempting to sell. We decided to record videos showing the different areas of the estate, thereby killing two birds with one stone—performance training and marketing videos.

After I explained the three fundamental rules of video performance to their team (don't stop, you can do it again, and the three-second smile), we went down to a lake on the property and planned on having one of the agents (we'll call her Jane) explain the different features of the lake while on camera.

Less than 30 seconds into the recording, Jane stopped what she was saying and said:

"Darn, I messed this up. Can I just start again?"

My response was swift and frank:

"Jane, our rule is simple. Don't stop. No matter what. I know this may sound odd or uncomfortable for you right now, but you must trust me here. So, this time, keep going, and do not stop."

Jane's response was typical.

"But you don't understand, Marcus. I'm just not good on camera."

Smiling big, I replied, "That's fine, Jane—but this time, don't stop."

She agreed and we then proceeded with the video. Although it wasn't perfect in her eyes, she got through it.

Over the next hour, we continued recording videos of different areas of the estate, with Jane being the main agent on camera.

After about an hour of doing this, we went through a section where Jane completed three straight videos, each taking only one attempt.

She was on a roll. Suddenly, she looked at me with a big smile and said, "Marcus, I think I may be a natural!"

Good for you, Jane. You're now on the journey of *The Visual Sale.*

Hopefully, you are, too.

 To see great examples of what you've read about throughout these pages, visit **www.thevisualsale.com.**

INDEX